Health Care Provision and People with Learning Disabilities

Contents

Foreword

Did you know that people with Down's syndrome are prone to hearing difficulties because of their relatively short and narrow-shaped ear canals and increased tendency for ear wax to become impacted? Well, if you are an established doctor, nurse or allied health professional you would think you should know such a basic fact, wouldn't you, to explain why people with Down's syndrome who consult you may not pay attention when you are talking to them. But, as health professionals working in primary care or community or hospital settings, it has been common to focus our interest on able people who choose to come to consult us. We tend to ignore the needs of harder to reach groups of people, like those who are housebound, have dementia, the homeless or – as in the subject of this book – those people who have learning disabilities.

So, has this stirred your conscience? Did you realise before I gave that example that those with learning disabilities may have a physical reason for being hard of hearing that you could remedy? Well, you should read this book – it is packed with loads of basic information about the physical, mental and social health of people with learning disabilities. It will make a difference to your everyday practice. The chapter on the communication needs of people with learning disabilities is particularly useful for all health professionals.

It will enable you to understand the difficulties that people with learning disabilities and their carers face, trying to access health care services through the normal routes. Looking at the NHS through their eyes you will appreciate the inequity that they experience compared with able patients.

Tricky areas such as gaining consent are covered – the legal stance in England and Wales for adults who have learning disability being the same as for those deemed to be competent unless proven otherwise.

There are plenty of tips about using non-verbal methods of communication to overcome difficulties so that you and the person with learning disability understand each other. After all, how can you do your job to the best of your ability if you cannot form a relationship and converse in a real way with people with learning disabilities? You need these insights from someone like Jo Corbett, the author, who has worked as a registered nurse in learning disability for about 30 years.

This book is a must read for all health professionals. You owe it to those with learning disabilities and their carers to learn how to practise at your best with all groups of patients who come under your care.

Dr Ruth Chambers
Professor of Primary Care
Faculty of Health and Sciences
Staffordshire University
and
Director of Postgraduate General
Practice Education
West Midlands Deanery

Preface

High-quality health care that seeks to identify and treat needs is something all of us hope for and should be available to all people, irrespective of race, gender or disability. In its reforms the NHS plan (DOH, 2000) sought to redesign health services responding to individual needs and transforming health care.

The needs of people with learning disabilities vary greatly, from those having mild learning disability, requiring very little support, to those with severe learning disability, having complex needs and requiring support from others to achieve all basic needs. This can lead to people with learning disabilities presenting a range of challenges for the people around them. During times of ill health these challenges will become ever more apparent. For the health professional working in mainstream primary and secondary care settings these challenges can be difficult to overcome when attempting to identify health needs and deliver holistic care that is responsive to their individual needs.

This book provides clear information and aims to assist mainstream health care providers in gaining greater understanding of people with learning disabilities to enable them to deliver the holistic and effective care that people with learning disability deserve. The reader is provided with information that emphasizes the range of achievements and individuality of people with learning disabilities and, through looking back at the historical perspective of care provision, illustrates the importance of improving upon the negative attitudes that can still prevail and at times lead to inadequate health-related decisions.

Sections of the book highlight many problems and barriers faced by people with learning disabilities when accessing health care seeking to raise awareness and influence improvements in care. People with learning disabilities will use health services at all levels and, recognizing the difficulty some mainstream care providers have when interacting with people who have learning disabilities, the book provides guidance to influence improved communication and support by health professionals delivering at both primary and secondary care levels.

Each chapter gives the reader information and guidance on dealing with a variety of situations found in health care settings. Examples of good practice are explained using case examples and experiences of people with learning disabilities and their carers. The book describes what is expected from the various health care teams and offers solutions to potential challenges and barriers facing them. It includes information regarding specialist support services that can offer assistance to the individual and to the mainstream staff teams, ideas are also offered on how to present information in a format that people who have communication difficulties can understand. For some considerable time, evidence has been presented that highlights the health inequalities experienced by this group, much of the evidence is explored and used to support the need to create improvements in care. Key legislation that offers a legal framework to protect the rights of people is explored and discussed in an attempt to raise awareness in particular about issues related to consent and capacity.

The evidence base for this book has been drawn from extensive research, personal experience, policy guidance, as well as from some of the current legislation that is applicable to this group. Since its publication *Valuing People: A new strategy for learning disabilities for 21st Century* (DOH, 2001c) has been the guide for those working to improve and develop learning disability services; its recommendations along with other government guidance are used throughout the text to help inform and remind mainstream service providers of their responsibilities to all patients.

As a registered nurse for people with learning disabilities, I have spent several years working in various settings and gaining an understanding of individuals who have learning disability and their families. Recently my time has been spent developing a greater understanding of health inequalities experienced by people with learning disability whose needs are often misunderstood by the mainstream health services.

Having spent time working with colleagues on a project that looked at implementing initiatives that were presented in *Valuing People: A new strategy for learning disabilities for 21st Century* (DOH, 2001c) regarding the concept of health facilitation, it became clear that improvements were required at all levels, including improved responses to health from within the specialist learning disability teams. For improvements in health to occur there is a real need for all services to work together in partnership with people who have learning disabilities and their carers taking a shared approach and responsibility for reducing health inequalities. It is hoped that this text will provide an additional resource that will encourage and support initiatives to improve the whole health experience for people with learning disabilities giving them greater opportunities.

My career has concentrated on provision of learning disability services in England in particular and as such the information presented largely reflects policy and legislation applicable in England and Wales. It is perhaps worth noting however that although there are differences in legislation as it applies, for example, in Scotland, many approaches advocated will be equally applicable to people with learning disabilities there and in other parts of the UK.

Jo Corbett

Acknowledgements

This text would not have been completed without the tremendous support and encouragement of my family, friends and colleagues. There are a number of people in particular to whom I would like to express my gratitude who have helped to influence and shape the early thinking behind this text. Caron Thomas gave me tremendous support and had she not have encouraged the writing and publication of an article along with my colleagues Maxine Prior and Rick Robson (Corbett *et al.*, 2003), it is unlikely that this book would ever have been written. I am eternally grateful to them all for their continued support.

Much of my career has been spent working with the people of Wolverhampton and thanks are extended to all of those people with learning disabilities and their carers who gave me the benefit of experience and knowledge over a considerable period of time. I was able to utilize it all when preparing this text.

A huge thank you is also extended to all my colleagues in Wolverhampton who were always, and remain, immensely supportive with my endeavours. During the later stages of preparing the text my newfound colleagues in Staffordshire have been a tremendous help. Special thanks go to Sue Jackson for the benefit of her experience and ideas and to Sarah Cherry for sharing valuable information with me. Thanks also to Kevin Elliot and Esia Dean from Gloucestershire for allowing the use of their valuable assessment tool and to the team from CHANGE picture bank for allowing samples of their work to enhance this publication.

A final note to Tony, Sam and Jack – your support and encouragement was brilliant and without it this work may never have been completed. I am forever grateful.

Understanding learning disability

1

Introduction

People who have a family member who has learning disabilities and those working in close contact through learning disability services will have a reasonable understanding of the terminology used; others express real difficulties in understanding what type of person may be referred to when seeking to define the term and apply it to describe an incredibly diverse group. There is often confusion with other groups in society in particular people who have mental health disorders. The lack of clarity about what is meant by the term 'learning disability' can at times extend to those working in the field of practice, as those providing specialist services for people with learning disability are known to debate who can access their services. This emphasizes how difficult it can be to categorize and identify this group of people.

This chapter seeks to give some insight into the various service definitions while also sharing the individuality and skills of this marginalized group. The chapter also offers a brief overview of factors contributing to a person having learning disabilities and discusses some issues arising from different attitudes held in society that can perpetuate negative responses.

Individual perceptions can lead to assumptions being made about the people for whom we provide care. It is perhaps useful to reflect on your own thoughts and feelings when faced with minimal information about an individual requiring health care support. Take some time to reflect on your own thoughts and perceptions of the group of people who have learning disabilities and who they are by looking at the question posed in Text Box 1.

Text Box 1

What are your initial thoughts when told that a patient with learning disabilities has been admitted to your ward or arrives in your department?

Think about how you feel about that person and how that might affect the care you need to provide.

What is learning disability?

Definitions

Over a number of years terminology used to describe groups of people has changed, usually with a view to offering an acceptable and more positive image of marginalized groups. During 1992, learning disability was chosen in preference to the then used mental handicap, as this was thought to perpetuate negative thoughts and images of the people who make up this group. Learning disability conjures up various meanings to people and is sometimes incorrectly confused with mental ill health or types of learning difficulty such as dyslexia. The diversity of the group of people who have learning disability also gives rise to difficulties in offering a clear picture of who would be included. The definitions that follow are presented in an attempt to offer some clarity and understanding for health care professionals to appreciate the skills abilities and value of this group of people.

Learning disability is therefore used to describe a group of people whose ability with intellectual functioning is significantly lower than that of the general population. This, when coupled with impairments in social functioning, gives rise to a variety of difficulties for this group both in understanding information and recognizing when and how to gain support in all aspects of life.

Valuing People: A new strategy for learning disability for the 21st century was published in March 2001 (DOH, 2001c) and offers the following definition to guide services with the implementation of targets within the document.

Learning Disability includes the presence of:

- A significantly reduced ability to understand new or complex information, to learn new skills (impaired intelligence), with;
- A reduced ability to cope independently (impaired social functioning);
- Which started before adulthood, with lasting effect on development.

(DOH, 2001c)

Prior to this the World Health Organization, Classification of Diseases (ICD-10) (1992) using the term 'mental retardation' defined learning disability as a condition of arrested or incomplete development of the mind, which is especially characterized by impairment, during the developmental period, of skills which contribute to the overall level of intelligence, i.e., cognitive, language, motor and social abilities. The cognitive impairment must have occurred during the period of cognitive development, which is most often taken to mean before the age of 18.

Intelligence quotient (IQ) has historically acted as a guide to professionals in the field of learning disabilities when determining the individuals eligible to access services, those who were thought to have an IQ score below 70 would be eligible to receive specialist support from practitioners within the field of practice.

Valuing People (DOH, 2001c) discusses the relevance of a low intelligence quotient (IQ), and stresses that IQ of 70 or below cannot be used in isolation in determining the provision of specialist health and social care. Assessments of social functioning and communication skills should also be taken into account. It is worth noting that many people with learning disabilities will not have had a formal IQ test and as such no score would be available.

There has been some debate regarding the benefits of labelling. Gilman et al. (2000) suggests that in some cases labelling leads to dehumanization and disrespect and for others the label can create opportunity and open doors. For the purpose of service development it may well be beneficial to group these people together under the same definition or label to allow for improved future planning. This should not, however, be taken to mean that all people in the group will present themselves in the same way; people with learning disabilities are an incredibly diverse group of individuals with a broad range of skills who at various times throughout life will require varying levels of support from staff teams and family carers.

In terms of supporting mainstream health professionals to understand and appreciate the diversity, along with assistance to recognize the patient who may require additional support to access the full range of health care, it is useful to look at the broad categories of learning disability. As previously mentioned, the person's IQ would have determined the level of service required. Although very few people with learning disability will have formal IQ tests linked to their diagnosis, the following descriptions can be used as a guide only to assist with general levels of functioning and skills a person has.

The World Health Organization (WHO, 1992) publication on the classification of mental and behaviour disorders (ICD-10) uses the term 'mental retardation' rather than learning disability and offers a brief description of the typical abilities. A person who will be described as having mild learning disability with an IQ score between 50 and 70 will be able to hold conversation, will be independent in self care, may have basic or limited reading and writing skills and will be able to maintain social relationships and employment. People within this group may or may not require ongoing support. Many of the people in this group will live independently with any deficits in intellectual functioning going largely undetected. For this group primary care teams will provide much of their health care with little need for intervention from specialist teams.

Someone with moderate learning disability will have an IQ of around 35 to 50 and, although achieving a degree of independence, will probably require support in a number of areas to do so. People who make up the group of severe and profound learning disability as defined by the WHO ICD-10 classification (1992) will require greater levels of support from others to fulfil all of their daily living skills. Their IQ score will be below 35 and they are likely to have very limited or specialized communication skills and a high proportion may also have additional physical or mobility problems.

A person with mild or moderate learning disabilities will live independently and in many situations will be fully able to make decisions about how they live their lives. As a health worker you may need to be aware that the person with mild learning disabilities may require a little more time and consideration to reach understanding about health-related issues. Use of language the person understands and explaining why things need to be done will ensure consent or dissent is achieved from a fully informed basis.

People with moderate learning disabilities will also enjoy a level of independence despite requiring additional support in some aspects of life. Again the health worker will need to take time to fully explain procedures. This could be done with assistance from someone who the person trusts although this may not be necessary for all. It is worth noting that the majority of people who have learning disabilities will fall into the mild to moderate category.

People who have more severe or profound learning disabilities will require a greater level of support to access the wide range of health care. They are also much more likely to have other associated health needs such as epilepsy or respiratory problems because of their condition. People with severe or profound learning disabilities need to be listened to and will communicate their needs in a variety of ways and are often reliant on others for support in most or all aspects of life including identification of health-related problems.

Again the level of support required is dependent on the individual. As a health worker it is important that you listen not only to the person but you also listen to family, carers and friends of the person to ensure every aspect of care and their ability has been considered.

Despite the limitations in skills described above many people with learning disabilities are having increased opportunities to participate and contribute skills within their community. Many people are gaining paid and meaningful employment that gives them a real sense of self worth. There are examples of employment opportunities within a whole range of services with people working in administrative and clerical posts, catering, acting, retail and many others. There are also several people with learning disabilities who are linked to sports with some excelling in their chosen area and competing in events like the Special Olympics. These opportunities for people offer great rewards for those involved and it is important that they increase.

Prevalence rates

Finding precise information on the number of people with learning disabilities in the population is difficult. *Valuing People* (DOH, 2001c) and *Once a Day* (DOH, 1999b) estimate approximately two per cent of the population will have learning disabilities. These figures can be explained as follows:

- Usually a general practitioner with a list of 2000 patients will have about 40 patients with learning disabilities, although there is considerable local variation.
- This 'guesstimate' includes children and elderly people.
- Of these 40 about eight will have severe/profound learning disabilities and the remainder will have mild/moderate disability, some of which will only have been evident during their school years.

(DOH, 1999b)

- 210 000 people with severe and profound learning disabilities and
- 1.2 million people with mild/moderate learning disabilities live in England.

(DOH, 2001c)

Whittaker (2004) explores the figures detailed in various Department of Health publications and points out that in studies mirrored nationally and internationally the number of people identified with the label learning disability who are known to services actually represents between 0.23% and 0.29% of the population. Whittaker (2004) goes on to question the need to seek out and apply labels to those who potentially cope independently of support from statutory services.

Although this group may be unidentified within specialist services we should not assume that as individuals they are accessing the full range of health care provision to which they are entitled. Many of the individuals will be living in the community with little or no support from family or friends. In many respects this group represents those who we assume have the necessary coping skills and strategies to make meaningful decisions and choices regarding their self care. However, many within this group will lack the literacy skills required along with an understanding of what constitutes good health; as a result of this, their health will suffer. Primary care teams are most likely the only point of contact for people with learning disabilities who have not yet been identified and will need to ensure improved access to the NHS is available when needed.

Within the health economy there is much that can be done to empower people to improve their own health. If we can get things right for people who are known to have learning disabilities, health care provision will improve for all of us, including those who may fit the definition of learning disability in *Valuing People* (DOH, 2001c).

However we categorize or define individuals within society it should not detract from some of the basic human rights that we all expect. It is important therefore to remember that people who have learning disabilities are:

- FIRST AND FOREMOST PEOPLE WHO HAVE THE SAME RIGHTS AS ALL OF US.
- People who will at times require health services.
- People who require additional help in various aspects of their lives.
- People who are individual with differing needs.

Factors that can lead to a person having learning disability

For the purpose of this text the following causes of learning disability are not intended to be all encompassing. The intention is for the reader to gain a brief insight into some of the main reasons for learning disability occurring. When offering treatments or diagnosis of medical problems there may be some relevance or link to the cause of learning disability, however, it must be remembered that the individuals are first and foremost people who will inevitably suffer from illness and injury at various points in their lives. Very few of these difficulties can be attributed to the person's learning disability, those that are, are often treatable complications that will require attention.

Social factors

Learning disability has no boundary and people from across all of the socio-economic groups can have a family member who has learning disability.

It is worth noting, however, that although prevalence of severe and profound learning disability is fairly uniformly distributed across the country and across socio-economic groups, mild to moderate learning disability does appear to have a link to poverty and rates are known to be higher in deprived and urban areas (DOH, 2001). There are a number of clear reasons for a person having learning disability although it is worth noting that in the majority of cases there is no clear identifiable cause of learning disability.

Prenatal and peri-natal causes

Prenatal factors are those affecting the development of the foetus before birth. The mother may have been exposed to infection or toxins such as drugs or alcohol. Viral infections such as Rubella (German Measles) in the early stages of pregnancy can cause severe learning disability with deafness, blindness and congenital heart defects. The severity of learning disability will usually be dependent on at what stage the infection occurred. Infection in the first three months of pregnancy represents the greatest risk to the unborn child. Since the programme of vaccination for rubella is now widespread across the UK very few cases of this type are found today.

Peri-natal factors are those caused at the time of birth or within the first 28 days of life (Watson, 2004). Birth trauma, lack of oxygen, or premature births can all result in the child developing learning disability.

Postnatal factors

A range of problems in childhood can result in developmental delay or learning disability as follows:

- Infections in childhood. Measles, meningitis and encephalitis can have an adverse affect on the development and sometimes causes learning disabilities.
- Accidental and non-accidental injuries are also known causes of learning disability.
- Toxic agents, use of lead in paints and other household materials were common factors although these are greatly reduced today.

Genetic and chromosome disorders

It is very difficult to state the proportion of people who have learning disability and the direct cause, but genetic and chromosome factors are estimated to be the cause in some 26.5% of cases (Craft *et al*, 1985). Watson (2002) suggests this figure is likely to have increased with the emergence of research into genetics and influencing factors (Knight *et al*, 1999).

Although there are several genetic and chromosome abnormalities that contribute to people having a learning disability, this text does not seek to encompass all of these in any detail. A brief summary of the clinical features of Down's syndrome and Fragile X syndrome is offered as these conditions represent the greatest number of genetic or chromosomal causes for a person having learning disabilities. For readers who would like to learn more, comprehensive lists of several genetic and chromosome disorders can be found in Mueller and Young (1998), Gilbert (2000) and Roy *et al* (2000). Additional information on learning disabilities and associated problems that could prove useful to the reader is also included in Roy *et al* (2000).

Down's syndrome

Of all the chromosome abnormalities, Down's syndrome is the one most commonly known and is thought to occur in approximately 1 in 650 live births (Mueller and Young, 1998).

Most adults with Down's syndrome have a moderate learning disability with about 10% having low–normal intelligence and would not be classified as having a learning disability (Roy *et al*, 2000). Children with Down's syndrome are likely to have speech and language delay and about 25% have features of attention deficit disorder.

There are a number of health-related issues for the person who has Down's syndrome that may require ongoing monitoring or attention. The Down's Syndrome Association (2004) have produced a useful schedule of health checks for adults with Down's syndrome. Some of the clinical features that could benefit from regular screening and monitoring are shown in Table 1.1.

Fragile X syndrome

Fragile X is a genetic disorder first identified during the 1970s. The discovery of the Fragile X gene in 1991 has led to the development of reliable DNA tests enabling accurate diagnosis and can also identify possible carriers of the syndrome. The availability of accurate tests has identified Fragile X to be the most common inherited cause of learning disability.

The learning disability is usually mild to moderate and in some cases will not be apparent. Those with the syndrome have a certain set of characteristics. Roy *et al* (2000) describe people with Fragile X as having a long face with a large forehead, large prominent ears, a large lower jaw and high-arched palate. There is usually some degree of social impairment, with social anxiety and avoidance

Table 1.1 Clinical features and monitoring for people who have Down's syndrome

Clinical Features	Monitoring
Thyroid function disorders	Annual thyroid function test is recommended due to a high risk of dysfunction. Test and treat accordingly
Congenital heart defects	Regular monitoring as required
Respiratory tract infections	Treat infections as required. Look out for sleep apnoea
Obesity	Health promotion/dietary advice Monitor weight at least annually
Skin conditions	Monitor and treat as appropriate
Increased risk of leukaemia	Monitor and treat as required
Hearing tests	Two yearly, also monitor for build up of ear wax due to narrow ear canals
Eye tests	Two yearly tests to check keratoconus and cataracts in adults
Muscular/skeletal. Atlantoaxial instability	May benefit from physiotherapy advice
Early onset of Alzheimer's disease (post 40 years)	Regular review of skills and ability recommended from 30 years to ensure baseline skills information is available prior to any deterioration

of eye-to-eye contact. Over 90% of affected men have large testes, but this is not apparent until after puberty. Self-injury is a relatively common feature, biting of the hand in response to frustration, anxiety or excitement can occur quite frequently and repetitive behaviours like flapping or waving of the hands are not uncommon.

Speech and language development is delayed with dysfluent conversation, incomplete sentences and repetitive speech. Hyperactivity is a common feature among boys with Fragile X creating further challenges for the people around them. Clinical features that could benefit from regular screening and monitoring are shown in Table 1.2.

Table 1.2   Clinical features and monitoring for people who have Fragile X

Clinical Features	Monitoring
Visual and hearing impairment	Regular testing/treatment of recurring ear infection
Attention deficit/impaired social function/anxiety. Self-injury	Behavioural therapy and advice
Epilepsy 50% of males	Regular monitoring of medication and seizure patterns
Aortic dilation/mitral valve prolapse	Treat as necessary
Muscular-connective tissue dysplasia Scoliosis	

(Fragile X Society, 2005)

Other conditions associated with learning disability

Causes of learning disability can also lead to other complications and or health conditions. Epilepsy is particularly prevalent in people with learning disability as are mental health disorders and autistic spectrum disorders. All of these conditions are also found in the general population but are found in increased numbers in the learning-disabled population. Differences in responses to treatments can also be noted and advice may be required to ensure appropriate action is taken.

Epilepsy

Approximately 30% of people with learning disabilities will also have epilepsy that continues into adulthood. This figure will increase with the severity of disability. People with learning disabilities are known to have poor control of seizures; this is thought to be due to the inherent brain damage. In addition, people with severe learning disabilities are not usually able to fully describe their experiences, and diagnosis may need to be made from information and descriptions of others. This makes it important to seek support and guidance to ensure all opportunities to improve seizure control are taken rather than accepting the situation.

The management of epilepsy in people with learning disabilities involves and requires the cooperative and collaborative working of the multi-disciplinary team, carers and users. Some areas of the country have introduced learning disability nurses with additional skills in epilepsy to support and manage issues arising from the dual diagnosis of learning disability and epilepsy (Doherty, 2003). These nurses will offer a range of support and advice to people with learning disability, their carers and other health professionals.

Cerebral palsy

Up to one-third of people with learning disability will also have a physical disability. Cerebral palsy is a condition that affects development of muscle and nerves. Although it should indeed be noted that not all people who have cerebral palsy would also have learning disability or impaired intellectual function, they may well develop similar health-related difficulties.

Individuals who have cerebral palsy are at greater risk of developing postural difficulties, eating and swallowing problems along with chest infections. They may require assistance from a broad range of professionals to maintain mobility and good health.

Mental health disorders

Social isolation coupled with a lack of meaningful activities for some can contribute to depression and other mental health disorders. People with learning disabilities are often reliant on others, leaving them with having less control over their lives in comparison to others. This can result in unexpected or unwanted changes for the person, such as moving to a new and different environment, residing with unfamiliar people, and having different people providing direct care. This could in turn be the precipitating factor leading to mental ill health.

Roy et al (2000) report that the diagnosis of mental illness in people with learning disabilities can be problematic, especially if the diagnosis is one like schizophrenia, which depends on the communication of complex subjective experiences to the examining clinician. Language skills may be limited or absent, depending on the individual's degree of disability. Doody et al. (1998) reported that people with learning disabilities are three times more likely to have schizophrenia than the general population. Despite this, access to mainstream mental health services for treatment remains particularly difficult. Various research papers suggest that this is due to the lack of communication between mainstream psychiatry services and learning disability psychiatry services (Moss et al, 1996; Roy et al, 1997; Hassiotis et al, 2000).

It is also worth noting that within the field of learning disabilities there is high use of anti-psychotic medication. Interestingly, Emerson (2001) suggests that these drugs are most commonly prescribed for challenging behaviours rather than schizophrenia, despite poor indications of their effectiveness in treating challenging behaviours and the considerable evidence of harmful side-effects of this group of drugs.

Autism

About 70% of people with autism have a learning disability and the prevalence of autism increases with the severity of the learning disability. Briefly autism can be categorized by:

- having poor social skills, avoiding eye contact and physical interaction, being withdrawn
- being delayed with communication skills. Speech is often repetitive and, in some cases absent
- displaying repetitive behaviours such as twiddling objects and hand flapping
- prefering to maintain particular routines and a having real dislike of change in their lives
- developing a particular skill in one area that can become all consuming, e.g. mathematics, music or art.

Many people with learning disabilities will have some of the above characteristics making unfamiliar settings and situations very problematic and stressful for them. Difficulties can be anticipated for some individuals when requiring health care, and preparation will be crucial for routine screening procedures. This could involve visits to a department and/or preliminary work to familiarize the person with the relevant department or clinic. The specialist community learning disability team will be able to support this if required.

Attitudes

When providing health care to people it is important to identify need through conducting a full and holistic assessment. Nurses and other health professionals will always attempt to do this, however, many health providers report experiencing a degree of anxiety when dealing with people who fall outside what they know to be the norm. When faced with people who have the label 'learning disabled', health care teams often acknowledge difficulties with providing holistic assessment and care (Grossman *et al*, 2000). This can be attributed to a lack of awareness, preconceived perceptions along with their own fears and anxiety about this group of people. In addition the busy environments many health professionals find themselves in may contribute to difficulty in responding positively and giving the time required in undertaking a full and detailed assessment that involves the person in a meaningful way.

Government documents dating back to The Jay Report (1979) have indicated that people with learning disabilities should have the right to live a full life with equal access to services as the rest of the population. The 2001 report, *Valuing People* (DOH 2001c) reiterates the same, with rights, choice, independence and inclusion featuring as a theme throughout the document. The document acknowledges that improving the lives of people with learning disabilities is a complex process, which requires a fundamental shift in attitude on the part of a range of public services and the wider local community. Generic or mainstream health professionals have yet to fully embrace this within their sphere of practice.

While (2004) suggests that the recent report, *Treat Me Right*, compiled by Mencap in 2004, provides a stark reminder that improvements in attitudes of public service employees is still required. The Mencap report (2004) details many health-related experiences. One reports a lady who, following surgery, was not communicating as she did prior to surgery. When this was discussed with staff they reported being unaware that the lady was able to speak! It would appear that a huge assumption was made in this case based on the label 'learning disability' with the resulting mistake that a cerebral bleed had gone undetected during emergency surgery and was only investigated days later when friends raised the question about her slow recovery and lack of speech. If a full account of the skills and abilities of this person had been undertaken and noted by all on admission, this would perhaps have been investigated much earlier. This account confirms the belief of While (2004) that low expectations of people with learning disability is often translated into unresponsive care, which leads to serious complications. While (2004) goes on to suggest that there is evidence to indicate that value judgements are made that frequently guide poor treatment decisions. While (2004) along with Mencap (2004) and others (Lennox and Dissens, 1999; McConkey and Truesdale, 2000) support the need for improvements in training and placement opportunities for mainstream health professionals, in particular opportunities to examine and improve attitudes, beliefs and values held towards people with learning disability is required.

Raising this topic recently with health professionals reveal some interesting anecdotes. On a positive note the majority of health professionals are supportive and would agree that people with learning disabilities should have access to the whole range of services. However, they acknowledge problems can arise when attempting to deal with individual cases. Some health professionals still hold the belief that people with learning disabilities should have access to specially trained doctors who only work with this group. Doctors who do specialize in this area clearly provide a valuable resource, but they traditionally focus on the mental health and neurological conditions affecting this group and as such are just as inclined to overlook the broad range of poeple's physical illness.

Historically people with long-term mental health needs and/or learning disabilities were placed in hospitals and various institutions that were to provide for all their needs. In the case of many, their physical health needs were monitored by hospital doctors who were often specializing in psychiatry rather than general practice. *Valuing People* (DOH, 2001c) makes this point stating that:

> Because mainstream health services have been slow in developing the capacity and skills to meet the needs of people with learning disabilities, some NHS specialist learning disability services have sought to provide all encompassing services on their own. As a result the wider NHS has failed to consider the needs of people with learning disabilities. This is the most important issue which the NHS needs to address for people with learning disabilities.
>
> (DOH, 2001c)

It is now clear and widely accepted within the field of learning disabilities that to move forward and to address the issues and barriers highlighted in *Valuing People* (DOH, 2001c), a collaborative approach to developing high-quality health care is the way forward. A sharing of skills and knowledge will move us closer to a more accepting and understanding health service.

Conclusion

Learning disability is a condition used to describe an incredibly diverse group of people. Although it may be necessary to categorize people to plan for provision of any specialized services, it remains important to view the learning disabled as people first who have an important contribution to make in society. This chapter has explored the terminology along with some of the reasons why a person may have learning disability and the potential effects that can have on health. There are a number of medical conditions that although not unique to people with learning disabilities, do occur more frequently. These have been highlighted to improve reader awareness.

More importantly the chapter has touched on attitudes and assumptions held about individuals who have been given the label learning disabled, and the effects this can and frequently does have on the provision of appropriate health care. There is, amongst generic health professionals, acknowledgement of the need to have greater awareness of the diversity and needs of people who have learning disabilities. Working collaboratively to support and meet identified health needs is now seen as an important factor in the continued attempts at improving the overall health experience for this group.

Models of practice

Introduction

Having an overview of the history of care provision for people with learning disabilities is important in understanding the prevalent social perspective and why continued change in attitudes within society is required. There are no doubts that major changes have occurred in the general attitude towards people with disabilities over the last century. This chapter discusses the move from custodial care that segregated people with learning disabilities to care that promotes independence and values the person with learning disabilities. Specialist learning disability teams exist to support individuals who have a wide range of needs; these services are governed by legislation and guidance that is continually changing. A brief insight into some of the key documents that have contributed to shaping contemporary service provision is offered. The chapter does not intend to provide the reader with detailed information but sets out to offer an introduction into the type of care provision that has been available to people with learning disabilities in recent decades. This information seeks to highlight the need for continued improvements in society's attitude to people with learning disabilities and offers some clarity of the roles of specialist team members who may be available to offer assistance to people when they use mainstream health care. The chapter also offers comparisons with person-centred planning and patient-centred nursing, these approaches appear to be consistent with the aims of the most recent government White Paper, *Our Health, Our Care, Our Say: a new direction for community services* (DOH, 2006) that seeks to provide personalized care for all that is available when needed and fits with the busy lifestyles people lead today.

Historical perspective

Current learning disability services are driven by models of practice that ensure that independence, inclusion, choice and rights are considered and available for all people with learning disabilities. These principles set out in *Valuing People* (DOH, 2001c) have still to be realized for many, however, when looking back, services and attitudes to people with learning disabilities have changed and improved dramatically in recent decades.

During the early part of the twentieth century institutions or asylums were developed to become self-sufficient colonies, catering for all the day-to-day needs of the people with learning disabilities who were resident. Atherton (2004) discusses the Wood Report of 1929 that advocated this approach ensuring people who were 'mental defectives' were contained on one site in order to minimize contact with the wider community. These institutions, often referred to as colonies, would provide accommodation, work, which could be in the workshop, farm, laundry or kitchens, and leisure for people who were diverse in character and had mixed skills and abilities. Using the Mental Deficiency Act of 1913 people would be admitted to the institution, often following requests from relatives. Two doctors were then required to assess and agree to the admission. The Mental Deficiency Act of 1913 categorized people as idiots, imbeciles, feeble minded or moral defectives; methods of testing against these categories were somewhat dubious and once given a label it was unlikely that this would be removed.

During the early part of the twentieth century policy was driven by fears that those people considered to be mentally defective were seen as a threat to society. Removing people from the wider community and housing them in colonies that were often in rural locations well away from the urban life was seen as a solution in minimizing the so-called threat to society as a whole.

As society became more conscious of human rights issues there was a shift towards the concept of community based services and social care models. In 1959 the Mental Health Act was introduced and replaced the Mental Deficiency Act of 1913. With this came changes in descriptive terms as well as making it possible for some people who had been detained or certified under the 1913 act to return to community. The National Council for Civil Liberties (1951) was instrumental in this shift in attitude, insisting that those classified as mental defectives deserved the same civil liberties, equality and rights as all others.

Medical models of care

Large institutions providing custodial type care under the auspice of local councils were transferred to the NHS at its conception in 1946. This promoted the notion that people with learning disabilities or – as referred to at the time – mental defectives, were sick and as such required looking after in hospital.

Medicine in the West, as Gates and Wilberforce (2003) suggest, aims to identify disease and disorders with a view to determine cause as well as enable preventative action or at least to ameliorate effects of any disorder or illness. Gates and Wilberforce (2003) also indicate assumptions of the medical model identified by Illsley (1977). Two of these highlight the view that people with learning disabilities were viewed as sick in that 'hospitals are seen as the repositories and treatment centres for the sick' and that 'physicians are seen as the key players in health care' (Illsley, 1977). Given that for a number of years throughout the twentieth century people lived and worked in hospitals, were looked after largely by nurses and the responsible medical officer made key decisions on their behalf, it is hardly surprising that the medical model prevailed for some time. Mitchell (2000) discusses the correlation of changes in the use of the term 'nurse' and the emergence of the Mental Deficiency Act 1913 contributing to the view that if you needed a nurse you must be ill.

Despite the changes brought about with the implementation of the Mental Health Act 1959 and the move towards community based services, the Act perpetuated the view that people with learning disabilities needed treatments and doctors to provide them (Gates and Wilberforce, 2003). Advancing drug therapies for the treatment of psychotic disorders were used extensively as the favoured treatment in people who also had behavioural difficulties. High use of these types of medication remains apparent today. Although this medical model of care focused on the mental health issues, there was perhaps a lack of emphasis on issues related to physical health with poor access to the range of skilled health professionals who worked within mainstream health services

It has now become clear that although there is a place for medicine in the care of people with learning disabilities, social models of care are favoured with an emphasis on ensuring people access to high quality health care as and when required.

Better services and community care

The next key paper to address the standards and quality of services for people with learning disabilities was the White Paper, *Better Services for the Mentally Handicapped* (DHSS, 1971). At this time there were still many people living in the large hospital institutions, some hospitals were homes to over 1800 people of all ages. Since 1971 there has been a steady increase in people with learning disabilities moving into homes that are based in local communities putting an end to the type of self-contained environment in the colonies that had become a way of life for many. By the late 1990s many of the large hospital institutions were closed and people with learning disabilities were transferred to alternative accommodation in a range of social care environments.

One area *Valuing People* (DOH, 2001c) addressed was the issue of the now much smaller number of people who continued to live in NHS-led accommodation. This group of people have continued to be denied access to primary care services and in particular screening programmes on the basis that they are being cared for by the NHS and as such would be under the care of a consultant rather than a GP. Many units that are still in existence are community units that were developed during the early 1980s to house those people who at that time were thought to require continued medical or nursing care. The units were based in the heart of communities with easier access to the range of activities and services that are available for all. NHS-led nursing and residential homes are also being consigned to history with the few currently in existence having plans to move people into social care housing or into alternative accommodation within the private sector.

Social models of care

Since the 1971 White Paper, *Better Services for the Mentally Handicapped,* the emphasis has been on social care with a recommendation that local authorities would provide increased numbers of people with residential and day services within local communities. Social services are now seen as the lead providers with specialist health care offering and providing services to those who need it.

Since early 1980s principles of normalization have been encouraged as the service philosophy with care providers attempting to provide homes as near as possible to everyday family lifestyles; this meant providing ordinary housing in ordinary streets with additional opportunities for both work and leisure from within the local community. This concept has evolved and continues to develop giving people with learning disabilities new opportunities to develop and realize their own choices and aspirations.

Person-centred planning

Providers of services, including those conducting community care assessments, are now encouraged to consider an approach that places the person with learning disabilities at the centre of any plan. Person-centred planning is about making the individuals' wishes and aspirations central to the decision-making process and creating opportunities to ensure they are included in any decision affecting their lives. People expect to be able to have choice in what they wear, what they eat, where and with whom they live, and every opportunity should be given to enable people with learning disabilities to make these lifestyle decisions for themselves. The government through *Valuing People* (DOH, 2001) sees person-centred planning as an approach that will enable people to live full and valued lives that takes account of choice, rights, inclusion and independence.

All services providing care and support to people with learning disabilities should be adopting these approaches with the aim of supporting choice, rights and inclusion. Long-term strategic change within learning disability services is the responsibility of local partnership boards; they have responsibility for shaping the future delivery of services. Person-centred planning as an approach is also seen as a way of assisting boards to bring about the broader changes in culture and practice that provides the opportunities that enable people to lead the lifestyle of their choice (DOH, 2001b).

Patient-centred nursing

There are marked changes in the way learning disability services have been delivered from the custodial type care that was operational throughout much of the twentieth century to considering and including people in decisions about their personal and individual needs. Similar comparisons can be drawn from looking at nursing in general. There has been, over some time, a move from the task-oriented styles of traditional nursing described by Binnie and Titchen (2001) to individualized and patient-centred nursing. The traditional model of nursing was a disciplined and routine style that centred on different nurses undertaking different clinical tasks with little time or emphasis placed on the individual needs of the patient. The individualized approach to nursing sees nurses allocated groups of patients with responsibility for supporting and meeting all their care needs. Binnie and Titchen (2001) discuss the limitations of these approaches for nurses and patients alike and suggest that patient-centred styles allow nurses to show greater respect for patients as people. Through offering guidance and support the patients are involved and offered choices about their care.

More and more people who have learning disabilities will have plans that are person-centred and will include their individual choices and needs regarding health care decisions. The patient-centred approach in health care environments will enhance plans and ensure that people with learning disabilities are included in their care. Binnie and Titchen (2001) point out that this approach allows nurses to have real human contact with patients and avoids the risk of categorizing or making assumptions about individuals in their care. They go on to suggest that this approach encourages nurses to listen and attend to all issues that the patient presents rather than just their medical condition. This is of particular importance to people from vulnerable groups like those who have learning disabilities, as often difficulties can arise that exacerbate the medical need. Examples of this are presented throughout this text with some ideas on how to ensure that adequate support and care is maintained. Where patient-centred nursing and health care is adopted in mainstream health services people with learning disabilities need to be included in this approach to ensure that adequate care is offered. In addition to this, individual person-centred plans should include information regarding support needs of people that prove to be beneficial for the person who needs hospital or primary health services and also to the staff team.

Current legislation

There are several aspects of legislation and guidance that govern learning disability practice. Much of it is the same legislation and policy that applies to all members of the population, with White Papers such as *Valuing People* (DOH, 2001c) targeting this group specifically and offering guidance to services.

A recent government paper that will influence and shape services is the White Paper, *Our Health, Our Care, Our Say: a new direction for community services* (DOH, 2006). This document recognizes the public desire for greater control of the type of care and treatment they receive and reiterates and builds on the choosing health agenda with the intention of services developing to ensure they are personalized and fit with busy lifestyles (DOH, 2006). Ensuring equity and reducing health inequalities experienced by all groups is a clear aim of health and social care services and is a constant theme found in a variety of recent government guidance. People with learning disabilities must not be excluded from initiatives designed to improve the health status of all. During the last decade a number of national service frameworks have been published with a range of services for various conditions. All recommendations within these frameworks must apply equally to people with learning disabilities.

Disability Discrimination Act 1995

There are a number of acts of parliament that are of significant relevance to people with learning disabilities. The Disability Discrimination Act 1995 offers some protection to people with disabilities in regard to employment and access to services. Amendments to the act in 2005 also place greater emphasis on public bodies to promote equality (DRC, 2005). Access to health care is known to be problematic for some people with learning disabilities and the Disability Rights Commission is currently undertaking a review of health needs and access to health. They issued an interim report of their findings in 2005 (DRC, 2005) with the final report findings due late 2006.

NHS and Community Care Act 1990

Services within health and social care are guided by the NHS and Community Care Act 1990, which gave definition to the roles and responsibilities of health and social care. Provision of community services is based on assessed need with local authorities taking the lead in this process, assessing needs, developing care plans, and arranging and purchasing care. Any services to be delivered must be based upon the needs of the individual rather than trying to fit people into existing services. In addition the act promotes equal opportunities for all irrespective of race, disability or gender.

The NHS and Community Care Act 1990 advocates and expects joint planning between agencies and has encouraged the development of a broader range of service to be purchased from the private and voluntary sector as well as those provided for within statutory services resulting in improved choice and opportunities for people in need of care.

Mental Health Act 1983

People with learning disabilities have a greater incidence of mental health disorders than the general population and as such are often subject to mental health legislation. The Mental Health Act 1983 is used and implemented as appropriate to enable assessment and treatment plans to be carried out. Approved social workers assess individuals and coordinate the process where application for admission is thought to be necessary. Where people need to be detained they must have a mental disorder as defined within the act and two registered medical practitioners must be in agreement that admission for assessment and treatment is an appropriate course of action. A person will be compulsorily admitted in order to safeguard the health of the person or to minimize any potential risk to the person and or others. It has been recognized that this act is somewhat outdated; an updated draft code of practice was issued in 1999 with recognition that extensive consultation was required. Updated legislation is currently being prepared and is expected sometime in the near future.

Mental Capacity Act 2005

This act will be implemented in England and Wales during 2007 after receiving royal assent in 2005. The act gives a much needed legal framework for those who lack capacity to make their own decisions and its application is discussed in greater detail in Chapter 4. This act is expected to clarify decisions where disagreements about what is in a person's best interest offering guidance and a clear framework for professional groups. Clarity in respect to health care decisions is expected with protection for caregivers where actions are deemed to be in a person's best interest. A draft code of practice has been published to assist with meeting the requirements of the act (DOCA, 2006) and at the time of writing is going through a consultation process.

Human Rights Act 1998

Human Rights Act 1998 contains 16 basic human rights that are taken from the European Convention on Human Rights making the convention effective within British law and offering legal protection in daily life. Professional groups working with people who have learning disabilities need to be mindful that any action they take must not undermine the rights of individuals under the act. Many people will be safeguarded with advocates working to ensure that the rights of individuals are secure. Further information can be found through various websites relating to the act.

Specialist teams for people with learning disabilities

Each area across Britain will have access to a team of specialists dedicated to providing services for people with learning disabilities. Details of one's local team can be found either through contacting local social service departments or from the primary care trust. These teams are likely to have variances in composition, but essentially they will all offer a similar service that is designed to provide support in specialist health and social care needs. All teams will be working towards implementing the targets set in *Valuing People* (DOH, 2001c) through supporting and acting as advocates for the people with whom they are working. In some instances this will include supporting and empowering people to access a wide range of services while also promoting and encouraging improvements in health.

Valuing People (DOH, 2001c) also advocated the need to develop and improve partnership working through developing integrated teams. Following this the task was set to review the role and function of community learning disability teams along with reviewing how well specialist professionals were working together and in particular how all the partners and stakeholders were included and involved (VPST, 2002). The review set out to monitor the community teams in terms of their effectiveness in delivering the key aims and objectives from *Valuing People* (DOH, 2001c). Since that time teams have either integrated or are in the process of moving towards integration. This will mean that in future all community learning disability teams will be expected to have a single point of access to their services creating less duplication and a more responsive service.

Access to learning disability teams is most often through an open referral system allowing any one to request assessment from a number of professionals. Core members of community learning disability teams are usually learning disability nurses and social workers who specialize in providing care for people who have learning disabilities. Other professionals working as part of or in conjunction with the team include consultant psychiatrists or those involved in the neurosciences, occupational therapists, speech and language therapists, physiotherapists and clinical psychologists. All team members will work with people across the whole care economy, statutory, private, voluntary and community services. Most teams will work specifically with adults who have learning disabilities although there will also be examples of children's teams or, in some cases, team members who work across the age range.

The guidance contained in the review toolkit for partnership working suggests the need to broaden the core membership of integrated teams to include housing organizations, employment services and primary care staff. In addition to this, users, carers and independent sector providers should also have greater involvement in the developing teams. To be effective all community teams need to be working to ensure that their service takes account of cultural and ethnic needs and is responsive to the needs of all carers and users.

A list of some of the team members follows with a brief description of the role they undertake. It must be recognized that each professional in the team brings a unique skill and professional knowledge in addition to those skills required and shared by all professionals working in learning disability teams. Some knowledge and skills are interchangeable, enabling team members to share tasks and alleviate duplication and confusion for people with learning disabilities and their carers. The skills and tasks listed are by no means exhaustive as it is very likely that team members will have particular interests and specialist areas of expertise that compliment one another.

Community learning disability nurse

Learning disability nurses are the only professional group to undertake training in this specialist area. They will have completed a minimum of three years study resulting in the qualification of registered nurse in learning disability (RNLD) or previously known as registered nurses mental handicap (RNMH). This group of nurses will offer a comprehensive assessment for a range of health-related issues, including health needs assessment and interventions that promote and encourage healthy lifestyles, advice on managing epilepsy, assessment and monitoring of behavioural interventions and health promotional advice on a wide range of topics. Learning disability nurses may also be involved in delivering therapeutic interventions such as helping individuals deal with bereavement and relationship difficulties and offering support in terms of counselling for carers.

Working in partnership with individuals and their carers to facilitate and encourage choice and independence is of prime importance. Planning, implementing and evaluating care plans are also key to effective work with a focus on person-centred planning and approaches. Along with *Valuing People* (DOH, 2001c) came greater involvement by the nurse in the process for health action planning. This can involve identifying health needs as well as offering one-to-one support to ensure that health care services are accessible to people when needed.

Social worker

Social workers are working to promote choice, independence through inclusion and ensuring that the rights of individuals are upheld. The international definition adopted by the British Association of Social Work is described by Bolton (2003) and states that the profession must promote social change, problem solving in human relationships and the empowerment and liberation of people to enhance well-being.

The NHS and Community Care Act 1990 is just one of the pieces of legislation that governs the community teams' work. The NHS and Community Care Act 1990 entitles a person to an assessment of needs. The social worker or alternatively the care manager will be expected to complete the community care assessment, and to arrange that the identified care needs are provided. People have incredibly varied needs and the social worker's role includes finding highly individual and specialized residential placements for those with complex needs, to arranging occasional respite care or finding day opportunities for clients and the carers of clients with learning disabilities. Following assessment the social worker, who is often the only team member with responsibility for applying for funding, will arrange for all aspects of care packages to be delivered supporting the clients with learning disabilities and their carers through this process.

An important role for the social worker working with adults who have learning disabilities will also be to investigate and monitor cases where there is suspected abuse of vulnerable adults. This could involve liasing with several agencies and supporting individuals through the process. Many cases will involve joint work to ensure full investigation that identify all aspects of care needs.

Occupational therapist

The main function of the occupational therapist is to promote and restore health and well-being through the use of meaningful and purposeful occupation.

Occupation, as defined by the College of Occupational Therapists, is the meaningful use of activities, occupations, skills and life roles, which enables people to function purposefully in their daily life. This relates to the performance of tasks used in all types of situations from skills used in personal care tasks to leisure activities and to employment.

Occupational therapists offer assessment and guidance for individuals and their carers for their daily living needs – work, leisure, and self-help skills. This involves assessment, advice on and provision of specific equipment and adaptations to their environment that can help to increase or maintain independence. Some examples of specialist equipment occupational therapists will provide are bath aids, eating utensils and advice on adaptations that improve access to and around the home.

Working closely with the other professionals occupational therapists enable people with learning disabilities to maximize their potential by focusing on their physical, psychological and functional potential by teaching or enhancing a wide range of skills.

Clinical psychology

Psychology is described by NHS Careers (2006) as a science based profession that studies how people think, act, react and interact. Psychologists are concerned with thoughts, feelings and what motivates people to behave in a particular way. They apply psychological theory and research in order to promote health and cure and prevent illness.

Psychological approaches can be applied to a range of difficulties including problems with relationships, depression, anxiety, obsessive-compulsive disorders, eating disorders, attention deficit disorders, drug and alcohol related problems and conduct disorders.

Clinical psychologists offer a range of therapeutic interventions and offer assessment and intervention that seeks to reduce anxiety, improve behavioural patterns and improve relationships between the clients and their carers. This is carried out through use of a wide range of psychological models and can include cognitive behavioural approaches, psychodynamic approaches or behavioural approaches to treatment.

In addition to direct client work, the psychologist also offers support, education, advice and supervision to other professionals in the team who have adopted a psychological approach to their work.

Speech and language therapist

Speech and language therapists are involved with the assessment and treatment of speech, language and communication problems in people of all ages. In addition they also work with people who experience eating and swallowing problems. Their role involves supporting people to communicate to the best of their ability.

Speech and language therapists working in learning disability teams use their skills to improve and maximize existing methods of communication while also providing advice and support to use alternative forms of communication. This could involve use of communication aids or developing skills in using signs or symbols to communicate needs. A major role for speech and language therapists working in learning disability teams is also to advise and encourage the development of accessible information in a variety of settings. This can involve training of staff, carers, parents and all others involved in supporting people with learning disabilities with their individual communication needs.

Physiotherapy

Physiotherapists are concerned with movement and aim to maximize the mobility of individuals, by offering health promotion and preventive advice as well of a range of treatments and techniques that enable rehabilitation. The physiotherapist will assess and analyse movement and function, using a range of skills, techniques and concepts in the management and treatment of physical condition. Treatment programmes will be designed to promote the individual abilities and to improve levels of independence.

Many people with learning disabilities require access to physiotherapy in the same way as the general population, for example, following injury, illness or surgery. In situations of this type referral to mainstream teams allows for access to a physiotherapist with the appropriate knowledge and skill to manage and advise on the presenting physical condition.

The physiotherapist working as a member of the specialist learning disability team will offer a highly specialized service to those people who have mobility and movement difficulties, in particular those people with profound multiple physical disabilities. Their role will entail assessment and advice on postural care including advice with provision of seating and wheelchairs and other equipment that aims to improve mobility or posture. People with cerebral palsy often require intensive input from physiotherapists throughout their lives to maximize their mobility and functioning. They will be involved with supporting developmental needs, teaching skills like control of head movements and how to sit, crawl and walk. The physiotherapist also has a key role in health promotion and risk assessment and will offer advice to carers about lifting and handling, to minimize risk of injury to themselves and the person for whom they care.

Psychiatrist in learning disabilities

Psychiatric medicine involves the assessment and treatment of a range of mental health disorders. The consultant psychiatrist will provide assessment and treatment for people with a learning disability who have mental health disorders such as depression, schizophrenia, dementia and behavioural disorders and forensic needs (Roy *et al.*, 2000). In addition they are skilled in monitoring and treating neuropsychiatry disorders such as epilepsy.

Psychiatrists working in the field of learning disabilities will often be called upon to offer advice and assessment regarding issues related to capacity and consent. This is done in conjunction with professional colleagues and carers. On some occasions it is necessary for the psychiatrist following assessment to monitor and treat a person's mental health condition under the Mental Health Act 1983.

Working jointly within the learning disability team allows for collaboration with psychologists and nurses and others regarding joint assessments. This creates possibilities for diagnosis and treatment for mental health conditions that may have manifested as behavioural disorders.

Conclusion

Society in the early twentieth century held negative views of people who fell short of what was understood to be the norm. People with learning disabilities along with those who had mental health needs and those who were considered to be moral defectives were certified and segregated in large colonies. To subject people to this kind of treatment that lacks possibilities for growth and independence is alien to the thinking of today. Looking back at the historical perspective makes us realize how much society has progressed in its approach to people who maybe fall outside of what is considered the norm. In 2006 there is greater expectation of respect for people for the individuals they are. Within health and social care choice, independence, inclusion and rights are now at the forefront when providing specialist services. This chapter has touched on the various legislation that has evolved and guided services, with the current emphasis on providing person-centred care that meet needs rather than making attempts to slot people into existing services that don't fit.

An introduction to the professional groups that offer support for people with learning disabilities is listed giving the reader knowledge of what type of support they can request. Mainstream service providers are required to adhere to the various acts of parliament and need to be aware of the guiding principles that govern practice. Mainstream health and social care providers can and should access the wide support networks available to people with learning disabilities to enable them to offer choices in care while also respecting the rights of people with learning disabilities who may lack capacity to make their own decisions. This will go some way to ensure that people with learning disabilities are always at the centre of decisions regarding their care.

People with learning disabilities have stood on the fringe of society for long enough. Fair and equal access to high quality health care that offers respect and responds to individual needs will support the principles of rights, choice, inclusion and independence.

Health inequalities

3

Introduction

Improving user satisfaction, choice and equity of access to primary and secondary health care services is a priority within all aspects of the NHS (DOH, 2003). This places a responsibility upon all services providing health care to develop responsive services for the total population and must include people with learning disabilities. The Disability Discrimination Act (1995) seeks to ensure that reasonable adjustments be made to ensure improved access for people who have disabilities. Within health care settings the adjustments required for people with learning disabilities are often in understanding, thought and awareness with some extra time for consultation being allowed as required. The impact of omitting these simple measures can have startling and damaging results not only for the individual, but also to those closest to them.

Houghton (2001) and Parkes (1996) identified discrimination, stigmatization and stereotypical beliefs as factors that contribute to the unmet health needs of people with learning disabilities, confirming that changes to these beliefs are required for health care to improve. A common theme throughout the literature on this subject concludes that health care professionals gaining knowledge and experience, regarding the needs of people who have learning disabilities, is crucial to providing high quality health care and improving the overall health of people with learning disabilities.

This chapter gives a brief insight into some of the potential problems encountered in maintaining good health and gaining access to the wide range of health services available to all. It also examines mainstream and specialist learning disability services and the reasons for health inequalities and introduces the role and concept of health facilitation as a way forward in reducing health inequalities.

Identifying health needs

People with learning disabilities are first and foremost people and as such are just as prone to disease, illness and injury as their non-disabled peers. There are, however, several disorders that occur with greater frequency in this group. It is not possible or appropriate to discuss a full and comprehensive range of problems in this text, but it is useful to consider the prevalence and incidence of problems that some researchers have identified as of specific consequence to people who have learning disabilities.

Respiratory disease is commonplace amongst this group and has been found to be the leading cause of death of people with learning disabilities. Hollins *et al.* (1998) reported that 52% of their study population were recorded as having respiratory disease as the cause of death; this can be compared to approximately 15–17% of the total population. Hollins *et al.* (1998) also reported that people with learning disabilities are 58 times more likely to die before the age of 50 than the non-disabled population. In some cases early death can be attributable to conditions associated with the learning disability although arguably many deaths will be due to late or generally poor diagnosis of conditions that can be treated, particularly when diagnosed early.

In contrast to the wider population coronary heart disease is listed as being the second most common cause of death for this group and is also found to occur in greater numbers than that of the general population (Carter and Jancar, 1983; Hollins *et al.*, 1998). Many studies also show that people with learning disabilities are more likely to be obese or underweight than other groups. Poor diet, lack of knowledge and choices, coupled with low rates of physical activity contribute to these findings (Messent *et al.*, 1998; Robertson *et al.*, 2000). This indicates a need for all health professionals who have contact with learning disabled people to be proactive in sharing information regarding healthy lifestyles and to develop health promotional material in easy to understand formats. Raising awareness will empower people with learning disabilities to understand and manage their own health needs.

Hidden problems can prove difficult to identify in someone who is unable to communicate in the conventional way of using a broad range of vocabulary. Some infections have been found through research involving greater numbers in people with learning disabilities. *Helicobacter pylori* is a bacterium that infects the lining of the stomach and duodenum. It is a common infection in the developing world and researchers have shown that it is found in increased numbers in people with a history of living in institutionalized settings. Wallace *et al.* (2003) found that the rate of infection in people with learning disabilities living in residential settings was up to three times greater than the general population. A case analysis, undertaken retrospectively, of deaths caused by cancer was conducted by Duff *et al.*, (2001). They found that of 157 people who died of cancer, 59 died of stomach cancer. An additional 25 individuals in the study group had perforated stomach ulcers listed as the cause of death. Duff *et al.* (2001) go on to suggest that undetected and untreated *Helicobacter pylori* is very likely to have been a significant factor in these deaths. Wallace *et al.* (2003) explored compliance to testing in their research and conclude that, given appropriate support from carers, people with learning disabilities can tolerate and comply with the test procedures required to confirm and treat this infection. For the person with learning disabilities, who has different ways of communicating needs, this infection had clearly gone unnoticed. It can cause considerable discomfort, and the indications are that in extreme cases death may be the final outcome, yet once detected, *Helicobacter pylori* is often easily treated with a course of antibiotics.

The disorders discussed above are also prevalent in the general population but are found to occur more frequently in people with learning disabilities. Disorders like respiratory disease can often be treated, and it is likely that late diagnosis and lack of timely treatments are contributing factors leading to early deaths in these cases. Other illnesses that would benefit from early diagnosis will inevitably occur in people with learning disabilities. This gives rise for greater vigilance on behalf of individuals, their carers and health professionals in identifying needs and supporting and encouraging access to appropriate health services in a timely manner.

Prevention and screening

Support to ensure that people with learning disabilities access screening programmes with the same regularity as the general population is also required to ensure that any problems are identified and followed up at the earliest opportunity. Where health professionals have doubts regarding capacity of the person to consent to screening, broader discussions are advised to consider whether additional support is needed to offer information in a way the person can understand or to consider what is in the individual's best interests regarding any screening or treatment plan.

Long-term health problems like epilepsy, depression and other mental health disorders are also prevalent in this group and carry the need for additional health care support from both primary and secondary care services. There is a need for mainstream mental health services to be responsive to the needs of people with learning disabilities and work is underway nationally looking at this using the green-light toolkit (Foundation for People with Learning Disabilities, 2004). The toolkit was developed on behalf of the valuing support team by the Foundation for Learning Disabilities to use as a benchmarking tool to enable services to identify which areas of mental health services are responsive and accessible to the needs of people with learning disabilities who also have mental health problems.

Barriers to improved health

Variances in the health status of people with learning disabilities are now well documented and there is a clear need to improve ways of supporting people to access a health service that is responsive to the needs of this group. In the White Paper, *Valuing People* (DOH, 2001c) the overall government objective for improving health is:

> to enable people with learning disabilities to access a health service designed around their individual needs, with fast and convenient care delivered to a consistently high standard, and with additional support where necessary
>
> (DOH, 2001c)

There is now a readiness in both specialist learning disability services and in mainstream health care to tackle issues that perpetuate inequalities in health for all vulnerable groups in society. It has been documented that mainstream health care professionals report a level of discomfort in providing care to people with learning disabilities due to their limited experience of providing treatment to this group (Howells, 1986; Lennox and Kerr, 1997; Grossman *et al.*, 2000). Acknowledging discomfort is a real step forward, however, all health professionals along with those working in health and social care environments need to recognize each others' limitations and work in partnership to break down the barriers that can affect the health status of people with learning disabilities.

It has been well documented over recent decades that people with learning disabilities have a range of unmet health needs. Howells (1986) identified significant deficits in health care 20 years ago. A wealth of literature to date continues to confirm that people with learning disabilities are two and a half times more likely than people from the general population to have some form of physical condition that warrants medical intervention (Van Schrojenstein Lantaman-De Valk *et al.*, 2000). Many of these problems are thought to develop due to lack of early detection and intervention. This could be due to a lack of insight or knowledge on behalf of individuals who have learning disabilities coupled with a reliance on others to judge whether or not one would benefit from visiting the doctor. Once it has been decided seek medical advice, negative responses are all too often found due to assumptions made by health professionals based on the learning disability label.

An illustration of this can be found in *Treat Me Right* (Mencap, 2004) where difficult behaviour is displayed and the doctor's response is 'these people do that sometimes' with little or no thought to further investigation for a possible medical cause. This particular man was later found to have a painful dental abscess, that when treated solved his problem; along with it the difficult behaviour subsided.

Diagnostic overshadowing

Diagnostic overshadowing occurs when the learning disability is seen as the primary problem, without considering other general causes of symptoms that occur and can be easily identified in non-disabled adults. People working in learning disability services see examples of this frequently, both in mainstream services and also in specialist provider services.

A community learning disability team received one referral from the care provider for a man in his late fifties who was reasonably independent and had always been continent. He suddenly started to get out of bed and urinate on the floor in his bedroom, and the staff team requested a supply of night-time continence pads, without first suggesting or supporting the man to visit his GP! On doing so he eventually received investigation, advice and treatment for an enlarged prostate. This man was receptive to the advice given and with help from his carers was able to adjust his drinking patterns during the day and was monitored closely for further signs of change. At that time he did not need to use any night-time continence aids to solve his difficulty. There was no real need in this case to involve the specialist community learning disability team. The support team working with this man should have supported the man to seek advice from the GP as soon as the problem was noted, and the GP would then have diagnosed and treated this as for any other man of a similar age with the same or similar problem. Instead of early investigation this man endured a period of time feeling embarrassed by his predicament, not knowing why this problem had occurred or what else he could do about it. Changes in patterns of behaviour should always signal an alert that all is not well; all those closest to the individual will need to reiterate this in an attempt to identify and where possible treat and eliminate any medical reason for the change in behaviour.

Another example of behaviour change can be illustrated by the experience of a woman living in a residential setting, who had always enjoyed meal times. Her appetite was good and there were very few foods she disliked. Over a relatively short period of time she began to refuse foods – the more her carers tried to encourage her to eat the more agitated she became. As time passed she inevitably began to lose weight and continued to be agitated and upset. By this time the agitation had extended to most of her waking day, probably due to hunger as well as discomfort. This presented challenges to the staff team and the friends who lived with her prompted them to seek advice. Her carers requested a health screen from the primary care team and after gathering information regarding the behaviour patterns and getting what limited information they could from her, she was tested for the bacterial infection, *Helicobacter pylori*. This proved positive and antibiotic treatment was given. She eventually settled back to enjoying her meals again, and her problem was solved. This case is a further illustration of someone with learning disabilities trying to communicate that she was experiencing some pain and discomfort. It also highlights the need for carers and staff groups to take swift and active steps to get to the cause of changes in behaviours. When presented, health care teams must take time to listen to all the signs and symptoms and offer their expertise in helping to reach a diagnosis. When these steps are taken it is often possible to offer treatment that alleviates symptoms and offers some considerable relief to people.

As previously stated, the evidence is quite clear that people with learning disabilities have greater health needs than the general population, however, a significant proportion experience difficulties and still do not access mainstream services. There are a number of factors that can explain this.

Ignorance

People who have learning disabilities are less likely to fully appreciate and understand the need to seek advice regarding their health and when they find themselves requiring health intervention the whole process can be confusing. It must be reiterated that not all people who have learning disabilities will react in the same way. Health professionals should not make assumptions, but should always check out facts and details about the client's understanding and awareness of each situation.

Some people with learning disabilities:

- may not fully understand the process of consultation;
- may not understand the importance of attendance at appointments;
- may be fearful of doctors and/or nurses;
- may be fearful of surgery and/or hospital;
- may have a low expectation of health. This applies to both the individual and the carers.

Text Box 2

What could you and your colleagues do to assist people with their understanding of health services and the importance of attending appointments?

Time constraints

Routines can be of significant importance for some people with learning disabilities, visits to the doctors or to any health professional are very often disruptive to usual routines and can cause anxiety and distress to some people with learning disabilities. Anxiety caused through lack of understanding of the situation and new surroundings can result in some people with learning disabilities having difficulty with long waiting times in crowded and busy clinics.

Offering reassurance and where clinically appropriate, seeing people quickly, will go some way to ensuring people with learning disabilities get the service required in a timely manner while also ensuring there is minimum disruption to the clinic or department. This will not only benefit the individual, but will also minimize potential stress caused by prolonged disruption to other patients and visitors who may also be waiting.

Text Box 3

A small number of people with learning disability will also have difficulty with waiting in crowded or noisy environments.

Consider the impact this may have on your department and on other people waiting for appointments. What can you do to reduce the potential difficulties?

Some degree of flexibility with appointment times could be considered for people who have learning disabilities, offering an early or last appointment or allowing time for a double appointment are options that could prove beneficial to all involved.

Physical access

Physical access in terms of use of ramps, automatic doors, lifts and any other means to ensure wheelchair access is available is what obviously springs to mind when access is discussed. There are, however, other aspects to consider to ensure services are accessible. For many of us entering a health centre or hospital, particularly for the first time, will be confusing. If a person has limited reading skills or uses a different language this confusion will be compounded.

Text Box 4

Consider the building you work in and how easy it is to find your way around.

Now consider how you would get around if you were unable to read or understand signposts.

Good signage around the hospital or health centre is important. Colour coding and use of pictures or symbols will be beneficial to several groups of people including those who have learning disabilities. Local self-advocacy groups can be instrumental in offering advice to those involved in planning and improving access to buildings.

Lack of awareness amongst mainstream health professionals

- Doctors and health care staff can fail to recognize potential health complications of conditions that cause learning disabilities.

Examples of this can be found across the whole spectrum of people with learning disabilities. People who have Down's syndrome may also have a range of needs that could benefit from regular monitoring (see Table 1.1). Thyroid function disorders are common although tests are carried out infrequently despite symptoms being apparent. People with Down's syndrome are also prone to hearing difficulties, due to shorter and narrow ear canals and an increased tendency for impacted ear wax. When health professionals are unaware of this, irreversible damage can be caused by inappropriate treatments (Mencap, 2004).

The number of syndromes that are contributory factors in someone having learning disabilities are too numerous to cover in this text, however, many will cause additional problems that could benefit from regular monitoring in the primary care setting. It is advisable to become familiar with the particular condition or syndrome in order to offer the range of health needs required.

Communication difficulties leading to inaccurate diagnosis

- Inadequate diagnosis and treatment for specific medical conditions including heart disease, hypothyroidism and osteoporosis.

Improved training and awareness for mainstream health professionals could help to improve this, as could a proactive approach to regular monitoring of health needs. Health professionals must look beyond the learning disability, should check on all presenting symptoms through discussion with the clients and their carers where appropriate and offer appropriate solutions as for any other patient.

Text Box 5

Think about a person you have worked with who has difficulty with communication, how do you gather the information required to conduct a full assessment of need?

How did you explain any treatments to them?
Who would you contact for additional support if needed?

When communicating with people with learning disabilities who perhaps have difficulties with verbal communication, it must be noted that their understanding of the spoken word can be greater than their ability to use it. Explanations regarding their illness and treatment plans may well be understood. Hand-held records should give details of communication skills, if not a family member, a friend or a paid carer who would be able to share this detail regarding levels of understanding, may accompany the person.

Less uptake of national screening programmes

- Fewer people in this group access health screening, such as breast and cervical screening.

National screening is an area where, all too often, health professionals and carers take the decision that tests are not required. National guidance on screening for both breast and cervical tests are based on the age of female. Women over 50 are invited for breast screening every three years and the National Health Service (NHS) cervical screening programme states that all females between 25 and 64 years should be invited for cervical screening every three years. Department of Health figures suggest that the uptake of the cervical screening programme in

2003–2004 was around 81% of those eligible. This compares to between eight and 16% of the population of people who have learning disabilities (Broughton and Thomson, 2000). Djuretic (1999) found that GPs expressed concern that examination was not performed because consent could not be obtained although the main reason given for not testing these women is based on their apparent lack of sexual activity. A number of researchers have expressed concern about this as women have been excluded from recall on this assumption, which is often difficult to verify. Many women with learning disabilities do engage in sexual activity and efforts must be made to ensure access to screening is offered for all and in particular those in the high-risk groups.

It is also concerning that GPs will not undertake tests due to a lack of capacity as individuals who lack capacity can neither consent or dissent from a fully informed basis. Decisions of this type need to be considered in terms of best interest and should take account of all those closest to the individual. Women who are able and agree to have the tests may also need additional support to understand what the test is for; Broughton and Thomson (2000) conducted their study and found that 36% of the women with learning disability who had had the test had no understanding of why the cervical smear was necessary. Parish and Markwick (1998) suggest that it is important to allocate enough time for giving information, and health workers may need to repeat information to ensure full understanding of the procedure. Guidance from NHS cancer screening programmes was published in 2000 offering direction for services to improve access and information for both cervical and breast screening for women who have learning disabilities.

Additional support through referring to specialist learning disability teams can allow for individual work to be done to help women with learning disabilities understand the positive and negative aspects of such screening. Similar work can be done to support men who have learning disabilities about self-awareness and examination and issues related to men's health. There are several booklets and leaflets available that can be used when sharing this information with people who have learning disabilities. (Health Scotland, 2002, Hollins and Wilson, 2004).

Lack of health promotion and accessible information

- There is not enough access to health promotion information in a format that people can understand.

Health promotion material in accessible formats is becoming more widespread. Information related to the 'Five a Day' campaign on healthy eating is now available in an easy-to-read format for people who have learning disabilities (DOH, 2005a) and is just one example of material that is being developed nationally. There are other examples of leaflets to assist with sharing information on cervical screening and breast screening that can be obtained through the NHS cancer screening programme (2000) web site. Hollins and Wilson (2004) have also developed a series of books on a range of topics designed to assist with getting the health message across to people with learning disabilities. Individually designed training packages and information leaflets are also being developed. Mainstream health professionals are advised to seek advice and possibly make direct referrals to their local learning disability team or the health facilitator for people with learning disabilities who should be able to offer support to patients who require specialist help and support to understand health related procedures. Speech and language therapists along with other professionals working in learning disability services are all vital in supporting people with improving methods of communication.

Lack of knowledge of care provider

- The carer or worker who is supporting the person who has learning disabilities does not have enough background information.

Encouraging use of hand-held records that individuals who have learning disabilities, their carers and health professionals can update is an effective way of assisting with improved communication. More detail on communication needs can found in Chapter 5.

Residential care staff should give health needs a greater profile. If a consultation is to be of benefit to the patient with learning disabilities, the health professional and the carer, it is important to ensure that clear up-to-date information along with health history is available to the clinician. This is of particular importance for people who need support communicating their needs and understanding the given response.

Primary care and funding arrangements

Mainstream health professionals in primary care settings are driven by a plethora of targets to achieve through the new general medical services (GMS) contract (DOH, 2003a). Many general practitioners (GPs) dismiss the need for a proactive approach to meet the health needs of this group through regular health screens (Kerr *et al.*, 1996; Bond *et al.*, 1997; Stein, 2000). When discussing the needs of people with learning disabilities in primary care some GPs and health professionals question the clinical value of offering regular or annual health screens believing that when presented with a person who has learning disabilities they will treat them as they would any other patient. This may be the case, however, the evidence remains clear that offering health screens helps to reveal unmet needs and allows for treatment plans to be developed and implemented (Wilson and Haire, 1990; McGrother *et al.*, 1996; Barr *et al.*, 1999).

Apart from a recent addition to the general medical services contract due in 2006 for developing a register, there were no direct financial incentives linked to the targets in the GMS contract (2003a) specifically for offering services to people who have learning disabilities. Debates continue regarding the appropriateness of any additional payments for primary care as a way to ensure improved access to health services. Many professionals in learning disability services argue that provision of adequate health care for people with learning disabilities should be available and that it is merely a change in attitude along with education that is required. Others perhaps hold the view that the additional time required to fully ascertain health needs warrants additional payment, particularly if it creates a willingness to offer an improved service along with understanding for this group (Benson 2004).

Within the GMS contract (DoH, 2003a) GPs are funded by achieving targets for numerous disorders all of which will be found in the population of people who have learning disabilities. Encouraging primary care teams to include people with learning disabilities in national service framework targets is one way of ensuring needs are identified. Greater effort must be made to ensure treatment plans are fully adhered to. This will ensure that income is generated within primary care while also improving health needs and equity in gaining treatment for people with learning disabilities.

Offering high quality health care for those with health problems will bring benefits to this group while also contributing to the new funding arrangements for general medical services. More importantly, all of these things indicate the need for all health professionals to be more vigilant in providing high quality health care to people with learning disabilities.

Health facilitation

One of the government responses to meeting and improving the health needs of people with learning disabilities is to ensure that health facilitators were identified. *Valuing People* (DOH, 2001c) suggested that health facilitators were required to ensure that people with learning disabilities are able to gain full access to the health care they need.

Maintaining health is something each of us needs to keep in mind. Many of us will have some awareness of what it means to be healthy and well. We will also take our own decisions about when we need to seek health advice, particularly at times when we feel unwell. People with learning disabilities may have difficulty recognizing these things and will be reliant on others to help them make health decisions. Visiting health care settings can prove to be quite daunting; for many of us it can be quite stressful despite knowing our visit is necessary. Some people with learning disabilities will need help, in varying degrees, initially to recognize the need to seek health advice, then to make the appointment and to get there on the correct date and at the right time and to explain why they are there and finally to understand and follow any treatment plan or advice.

Health facilitators for people with learning disabilities have the role of breaking down some of the barriers experienced by people with learning disabilities and, in order to do this, will be working with mainstream health professionals to raise awareness of health needs and the inequalities experienced. They will also be working with people with learning disabilities and their carers to empower them to speak up about their own needs and to manage their own health.

Carers, whether they be paid or family members, will be acting to facilitate the health needs of people in their care. Corbett et al. (2003) suggested that health facilitation should be considered as an integral part of the role of anyone with a caring responsibility for a person with a learning disability. The main carer, whether family or paid, will often be the person who identifies the need to seek advice from the GP or other health professional in the initial stages. Family carers have and do frequently act as health facilitators for their relatives in terms of recognizing the need to access services, support access and to assist with the follow up of treatment plans. However, the Mencap report (2004) lists problems experienced, often related to poor or negative responses from mainstream health professionals. Health facilitators, whether in a specific role or as members of the community learning disability team, will be well placed to support individuals and their families with any negative responses. Health facilitators and members of the learning disability teams are also available to support and advise mainstream health professionals in relation to caring for someone who has learning disabilities. As previously discussed, there is a readiness on behalf of mainstream health professionals to work in partnership with a view to offering an improved service to all patients who are in need.

Gaining full access to a service that is responsive to individual needs requires those working in health services to have some knowledge of the varied needs of all patients who present. All too often, health professionals fail to respond adequately due to the discomfort felt in managing the needs of people with learning disabilities (Grossman et al., 2000). Health facilitator posts have been set up nationally in an attempt to raise awareness specifically of the needs of this group. The role of the health facilitator for people with learning disabilities involves offering training and awareness sessions for mainstream health professionals and carers as well as working with people with learning disability regarding improving their own health needs and lifestyle choices.

Action for Health – Health Action Plans (DOH, 2002) discusses the need for two levels of health facilitation, level 1 required to support service development work and to inform on stratgic planning and commissioning in relation to health care and level 2 involving person-to-person work with people with learning disabilities. This will focus on individual needs, facilitating access and accompanying those who need it to appointments while also advocating on behalf of those who need it. It is the role often undertaken by direct carers and those who know the person well.

Primary care registers for learning disabilities

Health targets set in Valuing People (DOH, 2001c) include GPs and the primary care team being able to identify all people with learning disabilities registered with their practice and health facilitators who are continuing to encourage and support practices in doing this. Other targets set in Valuing People (DOH, 2001c) rely on having information in relation to the target group. For example, the Valuing People (DOH, 2001c) target aimed at ensuring that all people with learning disabilities are given the opportunity to have a health action plan is reliant on identification of those who are eligible for this level of support. Primary care teams need to have the list in order to be able to record details of their patients with learning disabilities to then offer a plan and monitor actions and outcomes.

Action for Health – Health Action Plans (DOH, 2002) indicates the need for audit and monitoring of initiatives designed to reduce inequalities in health; this again relies on identifying the target population. Practice registers that identify people with learning disabilities are vital and will enable teams, with support from strategic health facilitators, to monitor health status and uptake of screening services for this group. Information related to discrepancies and improvements are then shared with public health as suggested in the good practice guidance (DOH 2002).

Conclusion

The publication of Valuing People in 2001 (DOH, 2001c) has given services the impetus required to make significant improvements in all aspects of the lives of people with learning disabilities. Some of the target dates set in the document have passed but across-service work continues in an attempt to break down barriers and cross hurdles to build on the partnerships between services that seek to improve the health status of people with learning disabilities.

This chapter has looked at the range of health needs and the inequity in health services experienced by people with learning disabilities. Reasons for inequalities have been explored and the need for services to respond positively when working with people who have learning disabilities has been highlighted. The fact that some conditions can occur and go unnoticed highlights the need for greater vigilance on the part of all those who have contact with people who have learning disabilities.

Health facilitator roles have been developed both within primary and secondary care settings to work with mainstream health professionals to offer support and to share their knowledge and skills about the needs of people who have learning disabilities and to assist in identifying practice populations. An important aspect in identifying health needs is not to make assumptions about individuals based on the learning disability label but to see them as people first who may have an illness or condition. Diagnoses may prove difficult, but not impossible, and in many instances could be easily treated once identified.

Consent and capacity

4

Introduction

Inability to gain consent or a lack of capacity are reasons cited by health professionals for not carrying out treatments for people who have learning disabilities (Djuretic et al. 1999). This chapter will explore the changing legal position for treating adults who lack capacity to consent to treatment. With the imminent implementation of the Mental Capacity Act (2005) comes a legal framework and new Court of Protection designed to support the needs of those who require assistance with decision making in all aspects of their lives including health care decisions.

The chapter uses case examples of partnerships and understanding between mainstream and learning disability services and encourages referral protocols that ensure that people with learning disabilities are given opportunities to understand any proposed treatment plans enabling choice and control. Where consent is given it is from a fully informed basis. In addition to this the chapter offers some insight into conflicts arising when best interests and quality of life issues need to be considered.

When considering your approach to gaining consent it may be useful to reflect and ask yourself a number of questions that are listed in Text Box 6. Information that may give some clarity including the legal aspect are included throughout the chapter.

Text Box 6

Please consider the following questions:

- How do you establish competence to consent to treatment?
- How do you present clinical information to the person?
- How can you be sure consent is gained?
- When and how would you involve others in the decision making process?

Policy and law

Defining consent

Any medical, therapeutic or caring intervention that involves the touching of another person requires consent. Without this it is possible that the clinician providing the treatment could be sued through the civil courts for the offence of trespass to the person. Every adult has a legal right to agree to being touched and gaining the consent prior to carrying out any treatments will usually prevent successful trespass suits.

There are a number of ways consent can be given; written consent provides evidence that the person has agreed to a specific treatment. For the consent to be valid health professionals must give enough information to the patients that they understand the benefits and risks. Written consent is usually required for complex treatments, and the consent forms, issued by the Department of Health (2001b) allow for details on what information was given regarding the proposed treatment to be clearly recorded.

Verbal consent is equally valid, however, should difficulties arise, proof that consent has been gained will be much harder to establish. Minor procedures will usually require verbal consent. The clinician must offer an explanation of what needs to be done and why along with any potential risks of having or not having the treatment.

Implied consent can also be a valid format for the health professional to gain consent. Simply arriving at the hospital or clinic, however, does not imply that one is willing to accept any treatment offered. Examples of implied consent could be offering your arm to accept an injection or other actions that communicate your willingness to accept the procedure. Although this would be accepted in law as consent, it may always be preferable to explain your intention in order to gain verbal consent also for such procedures. It is feasible to conclude that offering your arm for an injection may be consenting to an injection, however, you would also expect to receive clear information about what was been injected and possible effects and consequences. When giving verbal explanations prior to gaining consent, it can sometimes be difficult to ensure full understanding is reached. Research that looked at women with learning disabilities who had had cervical screens identified that in some cases the women were unable when asked, to recall the reason for the procedure (Broughton and Thomson, 2000). From this one could conclude that greater effort should be made to ensure people are really clear about what they are actually consenting to, particularly those who have learning disabilities. This offers greater clarity and safeguards both the patient and the clinician.

To ensure consent is valid, information regarding treatments must be given in formats that are understood by the individual receiving the treatment. This can present difficulties when meeting the care needs of people with learning disabilities. Some people with learning disabilities will have difficulty understanding written information and communicating generally. This must not be taken to mean that they would not understand if time and effort is taken to impart information. Leyshon and Clarke (2005) suggest that nurses have an obligation to provide adequate information in a manner that is easily understood and tailored to individual needs. Indeed, this is reiterated in the draft code of practice for the Mental Capacity Act (DOCA, 2006). Mainstream health care providers may be advised to seek advice from colleagues in local learning disability teams or advocacy services when preparing any written or verbal supporting information for people who have learning disabilities. Working in this way will ensure all possible efforts to support understanding are made that will meet the requirements set out in the Mental Capacity Act 2005.

Mental Capacity Act 2005

In 1991 the Law Commission indicated that people who are mentally disordered should be treated as any other individual and, as such, are competent to consent. The burden is on the person alleging otherwise to prove it (Law Commission 1991). The legal stance in England and Wales for adults who have learning disability is, therefore, the same as for those deemed to be competent unless proven otherwise. The Law Commission went on to publish draft proposals in 1995. Since then debates have been ongoing finally culminating in the Mental Capacity Act 2005. Prior to this the law in England and Wales had been in a kind of limbo, leaving some individuals unable to consent to decisions and at the same time not having any specific framework for support from others to assist with making decisions and a need for reliance on application of common law principles.

The Adults with Incapacity (Scotland) Act (2000) came into force in 2002 and offers a legal framework for those who lack capacity for decision making in Scotland. In Scotland it was felt that previous legal frameworks did not meet the welfare and financial needs of adults who for various reasons were unable to make decisions due to their mental disorder or inability to communicate their needs. In the Scottish act any decision made on behalf of an adult with impaired capacity must:

- benefit the adult;
- take account of the adult's wishes and the wishes of the nearest relative or primary carer, and any guardian or attorney;
- restrict the adult's freedom as little as possible while still achieving the desired benefit;
- encourage the adult to use existing skills or develop new skills.

The Adults with Incapacity (Scotland) Act (2000)

The Mental Capacity Act (2005) was given royal assent in 2005 and implementation of the act in England and Wales is expected in April 2007. This will give a legal framework for those who have either lost the capacity to make decisions related to their own circumstances and for those who perhaps have always experienced difficulties due to their inability to fully understand the complexities of some decisions. The act gives some clarity to guide the professionals when acting in someone's best interests, with a new Court of Protection to deal with more complex cases and those where disagreement regarding the best course of action is in dispute. This replaces the previous Court of Protection, which dealt with issues related to the management of property and financial affairs of people who lack capacity. The new Court of Protection will also deal with welfare decisions including those in relation to health care issues of a serious nature as well as matters that are related to personal well-being. These were previously dealt with by the High Court.

The Mental Capacity Act (2005) is underpinned with five key principles that reiterate previous guidance and common law principles placing it firmly in statute.

1. A presumption of capacity – every adult has the right to make his or her own decisions and must be assumed to have capacity to do so unless it is proved otherwise;
2. The right for individuals to be supported to make their own decisions – people must be given all appropriate help before anyone concludes that they cannot make their own decisions;
3. That individuals must retain the right to make what might be seen as eccentric or unwise decisions;

4. Best interests – anything done for or on behalf of people without capacity must be in their best interests;

5. Least restrictive intervention – anything done for or on behalf of people without capacity should be the least restrictive of their basic rights and freedoms.

(Mental Capacity Act, 2005)

The presence of a learning disability must never lead to presumed inability to consent to all interventions. The Mental Capacity Act (2005) offers a 'decision specific test' that has been designed to assess capacity regarding a particular decision, lacking capacity for one intervention, therefore, should not lead to an assumed lack of capacity for another decision. Simply referring to the person's condition, diagnosis, age or behavioural pattern as a route to establishing capacity will not be acceptable under Section 2 of the Act. The Decision Specific Test is designed to ascertain the level of cognition and understanding of a particular issue and contains the points shown in Text Box 7:

Text Box 7 : Consent

The person has an inability to –

- understand the information relevant to the decision
- retain the information
- use or weigh up the information as part of the process of making the decision
- communicate a decision (whether by talking, using sign language or any other means)
- understand the information, even when it is explained in a way that is appropriate to the client's circumstances.

(Mental Capacity Act 2005)

Health care professionals have often lacked clarity about their role in assessing capacity and often prefer psychiatrists to advise on issues related to capacity. The Mental Capacity Act (2005) along with previous common law principles and guidance makes it quite clear that for medical treatment and examination it will be the responsibility of the clinician proposing and carrying out the treatment to ascertain capacity to make a decision regarding that specific procedure. They must record all their findings in the medical notes. Ascertaining capacity related to other aspects of welfare and or financial issues will be the role of the professional involved. Any disputes about capacity will be referred to the courts for a decision.

The act goes on to clarify information relevant to making the decision and includes reasonably foreseeable consequences of deciding one way or another or failing to make a decision, and the ability to retain relevant information for a short period only should not prevent an individual from being regarded as able to make the decision. This test needs consideration for each decision to be made and should be utilized to determine capacity in many aspects of life including health care. The act is quite clear that lacking capacity for one decision does not constitute a lack of capacity in all decisions. An example of this could be illustrated in the following case detailed at Figure 4.1.

Derek was able to consent to the initial investigations and was fully involved in making those decisions. When the tests revealed the extent of his problem and that removal of a large section of the bowel was required, resulting in the need for a colostomy, it was apparent Derek would have great difficulty in understanding and conceptualizing this and the resulting ongoing management and care needs.

In this case the health professional had doubts about the capacity to consent to the proposed treatment and Derek's best interests were considered taking account of his values and preferences along with psychological health, well-being and quality of life. Health professionals providing support to Derek had followed

---

Derek is in his 50s and lives with a group of friends in a small residential home. Derek requires support from carers to ensure all his care needs met. He has some verbal skills and is able to make his needs known. Derek became ill and was quite distressed and was able to let his carers know that he was in pain, this resulted in an emergency admission and the need for abdominal surgery.

Derek was able to agree that he needed to have a blood test along with an abdominal X-ray to find out what was causing his pain. He complied with this following help from his carers in explaining why the doctors needed to do these tests. The tests revealed a Sigmoid Volvulus. Treatment required major surgery to remove the large bowel obstruction with the additional need for a colostomy. Derek was unable to understand the complexities involved to enable him to consent to the surgery and having a colostomy. The consultant surgeon assessed him, making attempts to inform Derek of what he was proposing and why. Using the guidance in consent form 4 (DOH, 2001a) he was confident that Derek lacked capacity to retain the information and understand the consequences of having or not having the surgery and that it would be in his best interest to go ahead with the procedure. His carers were also in agreement and were made aware of the postoperative support needs. The surgeon signed the consent form along with a colleague who also gave his opinion. Surgery went ahead, Derek made a full recovery and continued to enjoy life, and with support from his carers he adjusted to life with his colostomy.

Figure 4.1   Case example – Derek

the good practice guidance in respect of consent, and had assessed his ability to understand and make a decision. Surgery was felt to be in Derek's best interests due to the seriousness of his condition, so they went ahead.

Capacity and duty of care

Jackson and Warner (2002) discuss difficulties arising when identifying capacity in general health care settings. They suggest that all post-registration doctors should be able to assess the mental capacity of patients, but many seem to find it difficult when faced with individual cases.

Health professionals and others working with people with learning disabilities are faced with daily dilemmas regarding care and consent. For some people with severe learning disabilities, individual routine tasks such as washing and dressing can prove to be traumatic. Reactions given to assistance can occasionally indicate lack of consent to the carer. However, within the duty of care, health professionals are legally required to maintain a basic standard of care for this group. The framework offered under the Mental Capacity Act (2005) gives further protection to those providing care where incapacity is established. Doctors in particular are required under common law to provide medical treatment to adults who are unable to consent or refuse treatment if that treatment is 'necessary' and 'in their best interests'. Doctors when faced with emergencies make frequent decisions of this type. Consultation on a multi-agency basis is advised as best practice wherever possible.

In Section 5 of the Mental Capacity Act (2005) provision is made to safeguard those providing care or treatment from incurring legal liability. Under the act actions involved in caring that could otherwise lead to infringement of civil rights will be exempt providing the appropriate assessment of capacity and best interests has been carried out. Tests will be carried out for individuals who lack capacity and are unwilling to cooperate with treatments such as routine blood tests required for monitoring levels of medication or perhaps thyroid function, if all those who know the person well along with the advising clinician decide it is in the person's best interests. Clear statements must be kept on file with evidence that decision-specific tests were undertaken to ascertain levels of capacity and understanding. Additional advice will also be required to ensure procedures are carried out safely with the least restrictive intervention and causing minimum distress to the person.

Consent and people with learning disabilities

Although no other person can consent for another adult, it is deemed good practice to record information regarding discussions with those closest to the individual. In particular records of why the intervention is thought to be in the person's best interest must be kept. (DOH, 2001b).

In 2001 the Department of Health issued good practice guidance on consent to examination and treatment, along with this four forms were issued for use when recording details related to gaining consent. The practitioner is required to complete these forms and offer and discuss any information, including benefits and risks, related to the proposed treatment. If there is a likelihood of additional procedures being undertaken, this must also be discussed and recorded as such. Where there are concerns about a person who lacks capacity, Consent Form 4, for adults who are unable to consent to investigation or treatment, should be utilized (DOH, 2001b) as in Figure 4.1, Case example – Derek. This allows people who are closest to the person to offer and consider their view about what they feel is in the person's best interests while giving the clinician clarity regarding the legal stance when deciding on capacity related to the decision to be made.

Doctors may be well advised to seek a second medical opinion for procedures of a complex nature particularly involving surgery. This ensures that a responsible body of medical opinion endorses the proposed treatment and offers further safeguards to all involved. Any decision made should involve the views and wishes of relatives and those closest to the person and should be recorded using the relevant consent forms issued by the Department of Health (DOH, 2001b). There will inevitably be disagreements at times about capacity and what is in someone's best interest and an application to the court of protection could be made in such cases where the issue of what constitutes best interest is disputed.

Working in partnership

The health professional proposing treatment must be certain that all attempts to ensure information has been communicated in a way the person can understand and, if appropriate, non-urgent treatment could be delayed while this process takes place. Use of communication aids, advocacy organizations and other professionals should be considered to ensure every effort to communicate the details of the proposed treatment has been made. In the situation for Derek detailed in Figure 4.1, surgical intervention was required urgently. However in the time available and following discussion with Derek and his carers, it was apparent that he would not be able to consent from a fully informed basis. The decision taken in the case example was perhaps made easier given the urgency to make a decision, as his condition was life threatening. This is not always the case in non-urgent treatments and as highlighted previously, some practitioners will prefer not to go ahead with treatments or investigations where they have difficulty ascertaining consent and/or capacity.

Everyday practice shows examples of people being denied access. Often this is due to a lack of awareness and assumptions made during short consultations. Poor uptake of cervical screening for women with learning disabilities can be attributed to health professionals making decisions not to recall due to the learning disability. However when asked individuals have been offered very little information regarding the value of and potential consequences of undergoing or not undergoing the test. The evidence presented by Broughton and Thomson (2000) suggested that women with learning disabilities were often unaware of what the test was for, and in a study by Djuretic (1999) GPs acknowledged that their reason for not undertaking these tests was linked to an inability to gain informed consent. Both of these studies highlight the need for clinicians to make greater efforts to ensure that information is shared to give people the greatest opportunity to understand procedures and why they are required. The forthcoming implementation of the Mental Capacity Act 2005 may see changes to this with an emphasis on assumed capacity and ensuring all attempts possible are made to assist people with understanding.

It is important to recognize that the time allocated to individual appointments may not be adequate to ensure information is absorbed by the patient. People with learning disabilities will benefit if they are given increased time during appointments; offering double appointments could be a solution to ensuring adequate time for sharing information and performing an examination. In a situation related to screening, additional time could be allowed for referral for further advice and support. If it is appropriate, referral to the specialist learning disability team for further educational sessions and support would go some way to making sure all efforts were made to ensure understanding of a particular procedure. In cases where the clinician decides the person is unable to consent due to a lack of capacity, the best interests of an individual will then need consideration. The clinical benefits of carrying out, cervical screening for a woman with severe or profound learning disabilities may be questioned. The clinician and those closest to the person will need to decide what is in her best interests and fully record the decision. If the decision is to not carry out the test, this must be reviewed next time giving further opportunity to explore need and to look at lifestyle changes that may have an impact on the woman's health. Historically there has been a tendency to not recall those deemed to lack capacity at three yearly intervals, but reviewing needs at each recall takes account of clinical need and potential for lifestyle changes and should be done.

In cases where problems are identified and there are uncertainties about capacity and consent, learning disability team members can often get involved. One example of this can be explained with the case of a 49-year-old woman who had identified a breast lump and was reluctant to visit the doctor. After long discussions with the learning-disability nurse, she agreed to see her GP who referred her for a mammogram. This resulted in the recommendation that a mastectomy was required. Her initial reaction to surgery was a definite no, largely due to her fear of hospitals. This lady had spent a considerable time in institutions and was reluctant to return to that lifestyle. There was a sense of urgency also with the consultant keen to offer treatment within a couple of weeks. The community learning-disability nurses who knew her well were able to spend time with her each day following her diagnosis, helping her to understand what treatment was needed and why. The positive and negative aspects of surgery were explained along with the need for postoperative care. This was done in conjunction with the breast care nurses and the consultant who were all skilled and familiar with the treatment options. A plan was drawn up and by allowing her the opportunity to ask lots of questions over a period of time and get answers, she consented to the treatment with a reasonable level of understanding of why it was needed and what the consequences would be if she did not go ahead. Support was given while in hospital and the nursing team on the ward kept her informed at all stages. Her treatment went well. In this case the alternatives would have been to accept her initial refusal and give no further treatment, or to have gone ahead without consent leaving her feeling powerless and not understanding what was going on. The extra time given by the learning-disability team allowed her the time needed to come to terms with the trauma and offered her the same choices as other women in similar circumstances. That time, effort and cooperative working between specialist and mainstream teams helped to make a very difficult time a little bit easier for her to deal with. Extra vigilance is required to ensure that people who have learning disabilities have clear assessments and statements that allow for self-direction where possible.

Services for people with learning disabilities continue to place emphasis on autonomy and respect. Care workers are also expected to make every effort to assist their clients to reach decisions for themselves, and to have respect for the outcome of that process whether individual staff or carers feel the decision is the most appropriate or not. Increased awareness of the concept of informed choice and the importance of this for individuals has led to recognition that both positive and negative choices must be respected at all times (Dix and Gilbert, 1995). This concept is further reinforced through the Mental Capacity Act (2005), stating that 'a person is not to be treated as unable to make a decision merely because he makes an unwise decision'. The Decision Specific Test (see Text Box 7, p. 49) should determine capacity regarding the particular decision being made.

Points to remember when gaining consent

- Always assume the person has capacity.
- Never assume individuals are unable to make a valid decision.
- Give all adults as much opportunity as possible to consent to any proposed intervention.
- Ensure the process of establishing consent is rigorous.
- Devote as much time as possible to communicating information to the person, seek additional help or advice from the specialist learning-disability team if time allows and it is deemed appropriate.
- The person giving information must be fully conversant with the treatment being proposed. Work in partnership and collaboration as and when appropriate.
- Consider 'best interests' if you feel the individual lacks capacity and is unable to give informed consent.
- Seek additional advice from those closest to the individual including multi-disciplinary team, carers and or advocacy workers.
- Record all your concerns and the process you have taken to reach a decision.
- Respect the decision of the individual if it is clear they have capacity to make that decision.
- Seek second opinion for more complex treatment decisions.
- Legal advice or application to the courts may need to be considered before undertaking procedures that have irreversible consequences.
- Consider all relevant legislation in particular Human Rights Act (1998) and Disability Discrimination Act (1995). Does your action contravene legal rights of the individual?

Advocacy and support

Most areas will provide high quality advocacy services that support people with learning disabilities in all aspects of their lives. This has been a growth area in planning and service development. With support a growing number of people are gaining confidence, enabling them to speak up for themselves. This includes sharing both negative and positive experiences of access to health services. People with learning disabilities and their carers are beginning to feel increasingly able to seek advice from health care professionals and within the speciality are being encouraged to request health action plans or screening from primary care teams.

Growth in confidence of people with learning disabilities and their carers will contribute to increased requests for support to maintain health. This in turn will lead to greater input and contact with this group by health professionals, and will eventually lead to greater improvements in health status and greater awareness and understanding of the needs of this group.

Ethical and moral considerations

When considering ethical principles Thompson *et al.* (2000) suggest that ethics is, amongst other things, a communal activity, applying rational principles and universal standards to social life. Thompson *et al.* (2000) goes on to define ethics in terms of what is good and right for humans with the general values and beliefs of society the basis for defining rules and regulations that we all aim to live by.

Moral and ethical codes govern our everyday lives through the various legal frameworks of the country and within our personal and professional boundaries. Nurses are expected to offer treatments that are impartial and accessible to everyone and as health professionals they have a responsibility to provide treatments to all within the resources available. This is laudable, however, Diesfeld (2001) discusses how people with disabilities are let down by legislation designed to offer them protection, particularly when subjected to medical interventions. Diesfeld (2001) suggests that the Disability Discrimination Act (1995) is often not considered where medical cases involving children or adults are brought to court; instead the principle of best interest is used. Diesfeld (2001) raises concerns that the courts continue to make decisions that have the potential to shorten the lives of babies and young children with disabling conditions.

Society continues in its attempt to identify and eradicate genetic and other impairments often using the notion of quality of life or what is in best interest. Chapman (2002) argues that it is incredibly difficult to define and agree an interpretation of quality of life. Pointing to the work of Albrecht and Devlieger (1999), Chapman (2002) suggests a paradox in that the negative perception held by the public is in contrast to that of the people who have disabilities who often report that they have an excellent quality of life.

Diesfeld (2001) cites a number of cases where end of life decisions have been heard through the courts stating that, where doctors have made clinical decisions based on quality of life and best interests alone, they are often in conflict with parents or carers, bringing to question differing interpretations of what constitutes quality of life and indeed best interest. Separating the medical condition from the disability can be incredibly difficult. Diesfeld (2001) argues the need for disability discrimination along with human rights legislation to be utilized in these cases. Although not applicable to those under the age of 16 it is expected that the new legislative framework of the Mental Capacity Act (2005) will offer further clarification seeking to provide greater protection to adults who lack capacity through appointing independent advocates to offer assistance in reaching the decision most appropriate for the individual.

Current practice in the learning disabilities arena is highlighting training needs of staff teams. Through presentation of research findings regarding health inequalities, changes in practice are happening, all be it gradually. In some cases mainstream staff teams ask why people with learning disabilities are given additional support to access health when other vulnerable groups are not! This widens the ethical debate where, for example, in acute hospital settings staff groups will be adhering to ethical principles by providing care within the resources available. Unfortunately resources often fall short of what is needed to provide the additional staffing levels that are required not only for people with learning disabilities but for other vulnerable groups. This poses a moral dilemma for staff teams who often acknowledge the need to provide greater support and care but are unable to provide them due to the budgetary and resource implications.

Government initiatives around choice and public participation (DOH 1999) fail to adequately address how mainstream staff should seek to include the needs of people with learning disabilities and other vulnerable groups The Human Rights Act (1998) promotes dignity, privacy, respect, safety and inclusive decision making. All these things should be integral within the NHS and available to each and everyone of us. Guidance notes in promoting equality and human rights in the NHS issued from the Department of Health (2005) suggest a human rights framework can be a helpful management tool. When placing the individual at the heart of services their rights and needs are taken into account resulting in a positive experience.

In ethical terms it would be both good and right to provide equitable services for all. In a modern tolerant society we should embrace those with differences, taking a caring role if required, but above all valuing people and affording everyone equal rights. In some cases this will involve offering and arranging additional support over and above that deemed the norm with greater emphasis on what life, quality and best interests mean.

Conclusion

We have discussed the problems that lead to people with learning disabilities experiencing health inequalities and at times what appears to be discriminatory practice. Government proposals in *Valuing People* (DOH, 2001c) set out specifically to improve the lives of people with learning disabilities through recognizing their rights as citizens, through making improvements in social inclusion, through offering real choices and giving the chance to achieve independence. Being given the right to access health care that offers choice and includes you in health care decisions are all helpful in creating opportunities to achieve a level of independence.

This chapter has looked at issues related to consent and how, through partnership working between mainstream health services and specialist teams, improvements can be achieved. Application of the new Mental Capacity Act (2005) should also cement the good practice guidance for consent issued in 2001 (DOH 2001a) giving professionals including those working in health care a legal framework to guide them in cases where capacity is questioned. Case examples show that following good practice guidance helps to ensure that people are given opportunities to be included in their care and as a result cope more independently with the situation in which they find themselves. Taking time to explain, include and listen to people with learning disabilities is of immense value and importance to them. Time in health care may be a very precious commodity, however, working collaboratively to ensure services offered involves people in their care and allows for decision making makes them feel important and valued as citizens who have the same rights as everyone else.

A number of people who have learning disabilities are speaking up by being involved in advocacy services. Many of them will tell stories of how they feel when the doctor or any other health professional asks their carer a question in preference to them. Many people with learning disabilities now feel empowered to speak out and ask 'please talk to me, remember I am the one that is the patient'.

Communication needs of people with learning disabilities

5

Introduction

Those of us working in learning disability services waited the arrival of the White Paper, *Valuing People* (DOH, 2001c) with great expectation and were encouraged by the content. The document expressed the government's commitment to rights, choice, inclusion and independence. Strong statements throughout reiterate the need to ensure that people with learning disabilities are given the same opportunities as all others in the community.

> The Government is committed to enforceable civil rights for disabled people in order to eradicate discrimination in society.
>
> [and]
>
> Promoting independence is a key aim for the Government's modernisation agenda. Nowhere is it of greater importance than for people with learning disabilities.
>
> (DOH, 2001c)

These statements give hope that the opportunities and life chances for this group will bring positive change and new ways of working in more effective partnerships. Getting it right for people with learning disabilities shows what can be achieved with and for one of the most vulnerable and socially excluded groups in our society. These and other messages from *Valuing People* are filtering through to the wider community including those in the health economy, however, improved attitudes and general approaches of society are slow to emerge and will benefit from an increase in pace.

Clear communication is one of the keys to achieving choice and independence, rights and inclusion. This chapter explores these four key principles.

In addition to this the challenges that face people with learning disabilities when attempting to communicate their needs, particularly, in relation to health are highlighted along with some guidance that will help to improve information exchanges.

Rights and independence

In today's society the legal and civil rights of individuals are deemed important and play a fundamental role in what we expect from life. We would all expect to have the right to a decent education, to grow up to vote, to have some form of employment, perhaps to marry and have a family, and to express our opinions on a range of issues. People who have learning disabilities should be no different. If there is a difference at all it should only be in the level of support required to achieve those goals.

Previous chapters have concentrated on health needs, however, it cannot be understated that the principles of rights and independence for people with learning disabilities need to be considered within the wider health economy. People with learning disabilities who require health care have the right to see the health professional who has the appropriate skills to diagnose and treat any presenting symptoms. They should also have the same rights and access to the wide range of health care as all others in society.

There have been a number of cases where health professionals make judgements on quality of life issues. One quote from a parent in Mencap (2004) highlights the denial of the right to treatment that could and does occur:

> The doctor came up and spoke to us. It took me a moment to realise that he was questioning whether we should go ahead with treating Victoria. He was suggesting that it wasn't worth trying to save her. He didn't know our lovely 33-year-old daughter and all the quality of her young life.
>
> (Mencap, 2004)

In this case the mother's response was clear, her daughter's life must be valued and should afford the same right to treatment as any other 33-year-old woman. The doctor in this case appears to be making value judgements without having a full understanding of the family unit or the individuals that make up that unit. Doctors' motivation for suggestions of this kind are unclear, particularly to those closest to the patient. Assumptions made regarding quality of life issues for all involved are possible factors; perhaps in this case the attempt, although misguided, was aimed at improving the carer's situation rather than the daughter's. Whatever the motivation may have been, the fact that the right to treatment for Victoria was questioned is a cause for concern and highlights the need for greater awareness and understanding on behalf of mainstream health professionals.

The Disability Discrimination Act code of practice (2002) points out that since 2 December 1996 it has been unlawful for service providers to treat disabled people less favourably for a reason related to their disability. Health professionals need to be mindful of this when providing health care. The Disability Rights Commission offers support in cases where discrimination and exclusion from services has occurred and is frequently involved in a number of legal cases involving service providers who have apparently discriminated against people because of their learning disability. Many of these, highlighted on the website (DRC, 2005) involve employers or leisure and retail service providers. Health care providers will not be immune to this type of action being taken where rights are denied due to the person's disability.

During the 1980s and 90s cases involving people with Down's syndrome who were denied life saving heart surgery were given media attention. Sankha Guha (1998) compiled a report for the BBC Here and Now programme. The report discusses one case where surgery was denied and another where the family raised funds and travelled to Canada for their daughter's treatment as the British consultant suggested the heart condition was inoperable. Despite this type of treatment being commonplace for babies who did not have Down's syndrome, some hospital teams were questioning the benefits of treating someone with Down's syndrome. This issue was also raised for debate in the House of Commons in July 2000 (Hansard Debates). Dr Brian Iddon highlighted the difficulties faced and stated to the house that discrimination of this type contravenes both the Human Rights Act (1998) and the Disability Discrimination Act (1995). The debate called for improved screening, faster access to health care, training for all health service staff and finally suggested that a firm message regarding discrimination against those with Down's syndrome should not be tolerated. These debates continue in the field of practice and on occasions, individual cases may require the courts to intervene to decide on what is in the best interest of the individual.

Adults who lack capacity to make a decision about a particular treatment are often reliant on those around them to make decisions based on what is deemed to be in best interest. In some cases there is disagreement between family and clinicians. Dimond (2005) discusses a case involving S, a young man with bilateral renal dysplasia. The court was asked to rule on the best interest of the patient. Dame Elizabeth Butler-Sloss, president of the Family Division held that the fundamental principle in this case was sanctity of life, as the proposed treatments for S were crucial to sustain his life. In addition to this Dame Butler-Sloss held

That just because a person could not understand treatment it was wrong to say he could not have it, it was crucial that S, who suffered from serious mental in addition to physical problems should not be given less satisfactory treatment than a person who had full capacity to understand the risk, pain and discomfort from major surgery.

(Dimond, 2005, p. 462)

This ruling, which allowed treatment to go ahead, recognized the right to life and that where life saving treatments are required equal treatment must be given.

In the case of babies and young children with disabilities doctors make decisions based on expected quality of life, and recent cases appearing in the press highlight this with parents having to fight through the courts for the right to life saving treatment for their child. Each of these cases need individual consideration, however, the evidence is quite strong that people with Down's syndrome and others who have learning disabilities are living full and active lives with increased longevity. Health care teams working with babies and young children would benefit from having a greater understanding and knowledge of the achievements gained by people with learning disabilities throughout their lives.

Choice and being included

In 2003 a national consultation concerned with choice, responsiveness and equity in the National Health Service was launched with key messages designed to improve the patient experience in using health services.

Choice needs to be extended to everyone regardless of where they live, what they can afford, their educational status, age, disease or condition, or cultural background. Designing services around the wishes and choices of different groups of patients will improve access to care and treatment and reduce health inequalities

(DOH, 2003b)

This statement along with others in the consultation paper clearly state the need for all people to be given choices. People with learning disabilities must be included in this. Achieving this will require improvements in information sharing to ensure that people with learning disabilities are included giving them real choices in planning their health care. Prior to this *Valuing People* (DOH 2001c), and the Disability Discrimination Act (1995) show the government's commitment to enforceable civil rights for people with disabilities in order to eradicate discrimination in society. The Code of Practice states, 'Since 1 October

1999 service providers have had to make "reasonable adjustments" for disabled people, such as providing extra help or making changes to the way they provide their services' (DRC, 2002).

This includes access to improved information in easy-to-read formats; without attempts to do this, people with learning disabilities will find choices about their health and treatment hard to make. One can also argue that the need for greater recognition of the needs of people with disabilities will go someway to making reasonable adjustments as stated in the Disability Discrimination Act (1995).

Person-centred planning is the approach advocated when supporting people with learning disabilities in planning their lives. This is explored in more depth in Chapter 2, however, choice and inclusion are key features to this approach. The person remains central to everything, being included and having their own choices and wishes central to the plan. Listening to what people want, however that may be communicated, is crucial. Specialist learning disability teams can then offer support to help people with learning disabilities reach realistic and achievable goals that they have chosen.

People with learning disabilities should be recognized as valued citizens who want opportunities to make real choices. Giving a positive approach and including all people irrespective of their disability in decisions about their lives is of significant importance if society is to improve its approach to people with disabilities. To achieve this an understanding of some of the communication needs and methods used will be of immense benefit.

Methods of communication

Text Box 8

Think about your ward/department and imagine being a patient. You have difficulty communicating your needs, you are not sure why you are there, you are afraid to ask and you are not sure what you can and can't do in that situation. Now, as the health professional, how can you help?

Communication is a fundamental need and is common to all of us, however people with learning disabilities are all too often incorrectly assumed to have no communication skills. Those people who communicate at a pre-linguistic level are viewed with negativity and often their carers will describe them as being unable to communicate. Hurd (2002) suggests that we need to start from the premise that all humans are able to communicate, despite the limited verbal skills, each individual will develop a personal, sometimes, idiosyncratic style. Hurd (2002) also points out that the onus for a successful communication exchange is firmly placed with the competent communicator.

When faced with people with learning disabilities the health care professionals will be required to utilize all their skills to ensure an effective and positive communication exchange takes place. Each individual will have differing abilities, those who have verbal skills may still require additional support or different communication techniques to ensure they have fully understood the information supplied.

There are a growing number of people who will have access to life plans or hand-held health records that are used as an aid to communicating health needs. Any personal information of this kind is designed to ensure all relevant and important information is available and will often be a crucial element in ensuring effective communication. It should contain information about how the person communicates and if there are any particular symbols, signs, actions or gestures that may be unique to the person, this should be indicated. If this information is not readily available the health professional may be well advised to establish availability of such information.

Text Box 9
What steps would you take to make sure communication is effective between yourself the person with learning disabilities and your colleagues?

Communicating using non-verbal methods

People who have learning disabilities with additional communication difficulties will often attempt to communicate in unconventional ways and may use a range of actions or behaviours in an effort to make their needs known. Ferris-Taylor (2002) suggests that a key principle is to recognize that people will be utilizing their best efforts to communicate and therefore it is useful to treat all behaviour and actions as meaningful.

Examples of behaviours or actions that may be displayed are all too frequently misunderstood. One man who was in hospital for investigation regarding renal function was thought by staff to not want a drink, as each time a drink was placed on his bedside table he would knock it over! What he actually wanted was the drink but required support to hold the cup. When staff placed the cup in his hand he was able to lift it to take a drink. This man, who was in his 40s had no verbal skills and also had difficulty with coordination. Reaching for the cup was his only way of letting those around him know that he was thirsty.

This example is particularly concerning as there were clear indications of renal problems and clearly fluids are a vital basic need for all of us. If a member of the learning-disability staff, who knew the man well, had not pointed this out to staff how many drinks would have been knocked over? Having access to the information regarding his coordination skills and support needs on a written admission form for all relevant care staff could have alleviated this problem. This example highlights the need for methods of two-way communication to ensure family carers, learning disability team members and mainstream health professionals have detailed information regarding the skills and abilities of people who have learning disabilities in their care.

People with learning disabilities may use a broad range of behaviours with a communicative function. Where conflicting responses occur to what is being communicated, an escalation in a particular behaviour is likely to happen. This can often result in individuals being labelled as uncooperative and appropriate treatment needs will go unnoticed.

There are several examples in literature and from experience that highlight the misinterpretation of different communication styles. The recent *Treat me Right* document (Mencap, 2004) details the story of a man displaying self-injurious behaviour, hitting his face repeatedly. His doctor is reported to have said, 'people like this do that sometimes'. His carers refused to accept this statement, feeling sure there was something wrong. They pursued this and when seeing a dentist found that their son had an abscess on a tooth and had clearly been experiencing extreme pain. Behaving in this way may have helped him to relieve the pain and frustration as well as letting people around him know that all was not well. Simple treatment with antibiotics at an earlier time would have resulted in pain reduction and no further face slapping. It is imperative to always eliminate any medical or treatable cause when considering behaviours that appear to challenge those providing care rather than just accept it because of the learning disability. Individuals will be using a variety of methods in an attempt to communicate something.

Speaking up through advocacy

Many people with learning disability are able to speak for themselves and with growing support from advocacy and self-advocacy groups more and more people are gaining confidence to speak up.

People with learning disabilities will report things like, 'when I go to the doctors they always talk to my mum'. Health professionals must be aware that when faced with individuals who are over 16 (and deemed competent), that they have the right to decide for themselves with regard to their health and any proposed treatment. This applies equally to people who have learning disabilities providing they are deemed competent and able to understand. Once reaching

18 years no one can consent on behalf of another giving greater need to ensure the person with learning disabilities has every opportunity to be included and involved in any decisions taken about their own health and personal welfare.

Caution must be taken in regard to consent with the onus left to the health professional proposing and delivering treatments to ascertain capacity to understand all aspects of any treatment (Mental Capacity Act, 2005). Carers on occasion may insist that their sons or daughters are unable to understand and will feel they are acting in their best interests. For some this will be the case. The general advice, however, will be to gather as much information as possible and always attempt to find ways to communicate directly with the person who has the learning disability. It may be necessary to gain details from carers; it is, however, important to adequately establish the level of ability and communication skills of the person to ensure that they are given the opportunity to speak for themselves even if additional support from a carer is required. With non-urgent treatment it would be seen as good practice to engage with the specialist learning disability team who may be able to work in partnership and offer additional support to the clients in helping them to understand any proposed treatments or conditions.

It would be helpful to offer supportive visits to a department or to develop individual information in a format that the person can recognize. This could be a photographic journey, a video of the department and/or procedure or it could just involve gaining the trust of a person who can be available to offer reassurance during any treatments and future visits. This may seem incredibly time consuming to a busy mainstream health department, however for the small numbers of people requiring this input, it will mean accessing an appropriate service that is caring and sensitive to patient needs and provides the most appropriate care in the best environment. It will also be possible for some of this work to be undertaken while the person is on waiting lists for treatment. For some, referral to learning disability teams will need to be considered and may be advisable when a referral into secondary care is proposed.

This approach would involve building partnerships and cooperating with each professional group to achieve a positive outcome for the person with learning disabilities, resulting in care being provided rather than refused due to the disruptive or uncooperative behaviour that could present.

Being uncooperative can often be interpreted as a refusal to consent to treatment; it could be that the person lacks the capacity to fully understand all aspects of any treatment. For many people who are unable to understand the full benefits and consequences of having a given treatment, they will be equally unable to understand the consequences of not having the proposed treatment. They therefore lack capacity to consent and dissent and in this situation the principles of best interest must be considered. Information regarding consent and capacity is detailed in Chapter 4.

> ### Text Box 10
>
> Think about the information you share with patients, what improvements could you make to ensure people with learning disabilities can understand it?

Guidelines for successful communication

When working with people with learning disabilities there are some basic guidelines to support a positive communication exchange.

Language

When communicating with any patient it is useful to consider the language used. The tone and inflection of your voice should reflect confidence and the language you use should reflect that of the individual being treated. This is of particular importance for someone who has a learning disability who may have difficulty understanding complex language. Any explanation about their care needs to be clear and concise, to the point and in language they can easily understand. It is best to avoid using abstract ideas; keeping explanations literal and focused will avoid confusion. You should always involve and include the person who has learning disabilities in all proceedings, seeking assistance from carers or advocates only if required. You should be honest and open with the person, giving them both negative and positive news as appropriate. You should also reassure the person with learning disabilities regarding treatments. It is possible that in giving an honest account of both positive and negative outcomes that people will focus and worry excessively about the negative outcomes, however low risk these may be.

Allowing extra time

When offering explanations you should be aware that the person with learning disabilities needs time to understand the information. Repeating the information and, perhaps asking the person to recap what has been said, will help ensure that the information given has been retained.

Consideration to waiting times would also go some way to ensuring a positive experience. Booking a person into the first or possibly last appointment and limiting their waiting time will, in some cases, help the communication process along and may avoid unwanted disruption to your ward or department and other patients who are waiting.

Information exchange

People with learning disabilities must be included at all times in any discussions regarding their care and treatment, however carers or other professionals who know the person well will be able to help share and interpret information both ways.

Where hand-held records are available, make sure the information it contains is used and acted upon. Any unusual methods of communication should be detailed and will help when working with individuals.

Non-verbal communication

Being aware of your own body language and acting in a relaxed, confident manner will be more reassuring for the person. Use facial expressions to back up verbal communication; a smiling face will always help to reassure people.

Personal space and contact

Some people who have learning disabilities may have difficulty recognizing personal space and may come too close. However, they may dislike it when you invade their personal space. It would be advisable to always use your verbal communication skills to make people with learning disabilities know you are approaching.

Offer clear and concise explanations about what you intend to do before making any attempt at physical contact. If distressed allow time for them to calm down, come back later to carry out the task if that is possible. Seek help from carers in explaining what procedures are needed and why, if you feel unable to carry out treatments.

Communication through use of signs and symbols

Always identify methods of communication and seek help from carers and or colleagues to interpret any signs/symbols as necessary. Sign language may be used as their main source of information. Some people may use 'Makaton' (Makaton, 2005), which has been developed from British Sign Language. Younger adults may be familiar and proficient at using these signs. Ask carers to offer assistance in understanding some key signs if these are used.

Use gestures and pointing to emphasize meaning with verbal language, pointing to relevant body parts. You could use pictures to support communication exchanges. If you do use pictures it may be advisable to double check initial answers to ensure the person fully understands the meaning.

Verbal communication by a person with learning disabilities

Levels of communication will vary with all people and those who have learning disabilities will have very varied level of skill and comprehension. It may be that some people are able to understand more language than they can actually articulate. Conversely, they may be quite articulate but lack skills to retain and understand the information that is offered to them. Some people may repeat words and phrases over and over or may use inappropriate language or speak out of context to the situation they are in.

If a person with learning disabilities is anxious or in pain, speech may become quicker or louder, alternatively the person may cease to communicate verbally or they could become monosyllabic. Occasionally people with learning disabilities may develop their own words sounds or gestures to express themselves. If this is the case carers should be able to help with any words or sounds that are unique to the person with learning disabilities. When assessing the person it may be helpful to ask for any clues or signs that will help the staff team with interpreting styles of communication.

Non-verbal

People with learning disabilities may either avoid or overuse eye contact and may be unfamiliar with the social boundaries relating to personal space or touch. This can create difficulties for those attempting to communicate effectively. Some people with learning disabilities may use their eyes to point at objects or pictures helping to indicate their needs. If this is the case you may need help from carers to ensure that all staff in the department are aware of any meaningful signals that will be helpful to know during their time in your care.

Unfamiliar environment

Health centres and hospitals can be very confusing places and it can be very difficult to manoeuvre around. The environmental factors and confusion is very likely to impact upon the communication. The unfamiliar environment can be frightening as can unfamiliar equipment. People will require reassurance and where possible may want support from their carer. Noise and other distractions can impair communications and this needs to be considered during communication exchanges.

Being in a strange place and not being able to read can make getting around any health setting difficult for example clients may become incontinent because they cannot find their way to the toilet. It is useful to consider visual methods and signposting that are used to help people navigate their way around the building.

People with learning disabilities may communicate using a range of behaviours. For example, if clients find waiting difficult or are anxious about the appointment, they may become agitated and display uncooperative or difficult to manage behaviours. Not being able to fully understand the need and benefits of treatments can also lead to difficulties. Preparation well before the actual appointment date could help to alleviate this.

Where to get help

Health departments may find it helpful to seek advice from colleagues in learning disability services who are well placed to offer advice and will on occasions be available to give some direct assistance. Your local learning disability team will have skills and knowledge as well as access to a range of resources to assist with improving the communication needs of people with learning disabilities. You could make contact and find out about referral protocols and the help that can be available.

Working in partnership to improve the health experience through sharing skills and listening to each other will go some way to improving the health of people with learning disabilities.

Accessible information

Health-related information is available in abundance, health promotion campaigns produce leaflets for the population, posters are placed on the wall in health clinics and health-related information is to be found in the media through television or magazines. Much of this information will be of little or no use to people with learning disabilities who cannot read or filter information that may be of relevance to them. This area is of huge importance and must be considered in mainstream health settings. If no consideration to how this information is disseminated, to not only prevent, but also to explain a condition, the health inequalities of this group will continue.

There are, available through a number of sources, a growing number of pictures and resources designed to assist with developing information in formats that are easier to understand (CHANGE Picture Bank, photo symbols). To ensure that people with learning disabilities are able to access the right information for them, individually designed information will be the most effective approach. This will involve working with those who know the client best, looking at the information used in mainstream healthcare and adapting it using the available tools and resources. Other approaches may involve developing accessible information for all, however, the individuality of people with learning disabilities means that specific individual approaches will give increased opportunities to understand information.

Development of accessible information is taking place both at an individual level and nationally. Samples of accessible information to support the process of health promotion along with accessible versions of documents that relate to people with learning disabilities are now expected and developed. *Valuing People* (DOH, 2001c) was published with an accessible version and included audiotapes to help people with learning disabilities understand what the government objectives were for improving services available to them. Leaflets explaining consent, cervical screening and dietary advice have all been developed in easy-to-read formats using simple language and pictures to assist with getting the

(a)

MY HEALTH RECORD & PLAN

Name....................................

(Pictures reproduced with permission from CHANGE Picture Bank)

(b)

Things I need to stay healthy	Things I need to do	Who can help me and when	Is it being done?
Eating and drinking	Eat more vegetables and fruit	My Mom Every day	Yes

(Pictures reproduced with permission from CHANGE Picture Bank)

Figure 5.1 CHANGE Picture Bank-photo symbols

information to those who need it. These are available from Department of Health publications.

Use of computer technology is widely available in learning disability services and access to various software packages with a range of pictures and symbols creates opportunities to individualize information for people. CHANGE Picture Bank (2004) is a collection of drawings devised and developed with and by people with learning disabilities that have been used extensively in government documents and by services when preparing information such as minutes of meetings or consultation documents. In addition these pictures along with photographic or other symbols are used to support information in individually designed hand-held records and person-centred plans. Examples of how CHANGE pictures are used to build the health action plan can be seen in Figure 5.1, a & b. The health picture bank offers a range of images that include medication, drawings that depict situations and those that reflect healthy lifestyles. An alternative approach to using drawings would be to use actual photographs of people or places with which the person is aware or familiar.

Conclusion

Britain's diverse population uses many languages and it is largely accepted within health service departments that information needs to be developed in languages other than English to ensure that minority ethnic groups have access to information. Much of the public health information and health promoting leaflets are already available in a variety of languages and many services will also have access to interpreters to assist with translating when required. Department of Health information is now being developed to meet the needs of people with learning disabilities. There is also a wealth of resources to support the development of accessible information in formats that people with learning disabilities can understand, however, it is not yet common practice in mainstream services to support their communication needs. Building partnerships between specialist learning disabilities teams and mainstream health teams can help to improve this.

This chapter has explored the need to ensure that all people with learning disabilities are given the same rights as others in society and has explored examples of discrimination and assumptions about people that can and often do lead to denied rights.

For health teams caring for someone either as an in-patient or in a clinic it is important to ensure that the person who has learning disabilities is included in all consultations and that all efforts to explain procedures are taken. Where possible forward planning will be of immense benefit, including involvement from the community learning disability team who may be able to work with the person to help prepare for appointments and any screening procedures. Being in good health and being given the opportunity to access high quality health care when needed will also offer people with learning disabilities improved chances of reaching a level of independence.

Good communication is key and often the health professional will need to use a range of options to ensure that they and the person with learning disabilities understand each other. The chapter has also offered guidance to support positive interactions between the individual with learning disabilities and the mainstream health care team.

Roles and responsibilities of carers

6

Introduction

Many people with learning disabilities are reliant on others to provide some level of support whether for short periods of time during the day or for the full 24 hours. Supporting people with their care needs involves a high level of commitment and responsibility on behalf of the carer and is a role of vital importance. The needs of family carers along with the introduction of legislation related to carers is explored in this chapter highlighting the need for recognition of the valuable contribution they make in their caring role. People, often family members, who provide a substantial amount of support are entitled to carer assessments that take account of their own health needs and aspirations and need to be advised of their entitlement. This chapter also looks at utilising the valuable expertise gained as carers through involving them in delivering educational programmes to staff teams, in addition to this suggestions for gaining and using their views to develop and enhance services.

Other aspects of care are also explored through specialist care providers and particularly their role supporting people with learning disabilities and meeting their health needs. Paid carers supporting direct care needs often have the same level of responsibility as family carers for ensuring the health needs of the people with learning disabilities in their care. The chapter offers some practical guidance aimed at all carers in their role as caregivers. In addition to this a checklist of questions to help prepare carers for accompanying people with learning disabilities to appointments with health professionals is included, with the intention of maximising the potential for positive outcomes from any consultation. People with learning disabilities are often reliant on others to offer assistance that supports their health needs, the role of carers is of vital importance in the quest to reduce the health inequalities experienced by this group of people.

Carers

Carers are people who provide for a wide range of support needs to other people and will fall into a number of categories. Parents provide care and support for their children. This role changes as children develop a level of independence and they move into adulthood. For some, however, their caring role will continue if their child has or develops special needs. Others will care for an elderly parent or for someone following injury or illness. Throughout England and Wales there are approximately 5.2 million carers with a high proportion of these spending 50 hours or more on their caring role (DOH, 2005b) This figure increases daily with more and more people taking on substantial caring roles for family members, neighbours or friends.

Legislation is in place that offers a framework for support for carers in the form of Carers and Disabled Children Act 2000 and Carers (Equal Opportunities) Act, 2004. This entitles carers to assess their own needs recognizing the valued role they play. Although family carers make up a high proportion of carers, there are also huge numbers of people providing care in different types of paid employment. The Commission for Social Care Inspection has the responsibility for inspecting, assessing and reviewing care services across England, and at this time has in excess of 26,000 care establishments registered on the web site (CSCI, 2006) which illustrates the considerable numbers of staff required to meet care needs.

One aspect of the role of all carers providing support should be to take account of supporting the person or people they care for to maintain their health and access services when they need it. Carers' needs and approach to the role will differ depending on whether they are employed or acting as family carers.

Not all carers who offer substantial unpaid support to others are family, however the term family carer is used throughout the chapter to reflect the army of carers providing crucial support to people that often enables them to remain in the family home or place of their choice. They also benefit from the legislation.

Family carers

There is no doubt that people who act in a caring role provide a vital service to those who need it. Carers are in a unique position assisting the people for whom they care with various aspects of self care. They also act on their behalf as and when necessary. Provision of health care support and helping a person to recognize the need for health intervention is an extremely important aspect of the role of carer. For people with learning disabilities there is wide recognition that health care support can fall short of that which many of us expect. Carers, whether they are family or paid, should be at the forefront in supporting both recognition of health needs and access to the relevant service.

Many people with learning disabilities require some level of support in their daily lives and as such will need other people to provide or ensure their care needs are met. As many as 60% of people who have learning disabilities reside with family carers and of these some 20% will be living with a family carer who is 70 or over (DOH, 2001c). Collectively these family carers provide wide ranging and vital support networks for people who have learning disabilities. Various government documents acknowledge that without the support and contribution from the network of family carers local health and social care services would find it very difficult to provide adequate care for this group. *Valuing People* (DOH, 2001c) recognized the valuable contribution carers of people with learning disabilities make and advocated a number of improvements that would recognise and support their efforts. Carers need to have access to more information and improved assessment of their own needs. Greater access to short breaks is required, and carers need to be viewed as valued partners working with the statutory organizations. Carers are now included as key members on local learning disability partnership boards and other groups and their views are seen as both important and influential in service developments.

Guidance and legislation for carers

Legislation was first introduced to support the needs of individuals who provide a substantial amount of care to another person on a regular basis. This came in the form of The Carers (Recognition and Services) Act, 1995. This act gave carers a legal status and recognized their rights. People providing care on a regular basis are entitled under the act to request an assessment. This assessment includes their ability to provide and continue with their caring role and is independent from the assessed needs of the person being cared for. Once completed, however, social service departments are expected to take outcomes of the assessment into account when determining service provision for the cared-for person.

Further changes that update the legislation came with the implementation of the Carers and Disabled Children Act, 2000. This act gave local authorities the ability to offer support to carers that enables them to ensure their own health and well-being is maintained. Carers are defined under the 2000 Act as people with parental responsibility for disabled children who are aged 16 and over. The Carers and Disabled Children Act, 2000 gives carers the right to an assessment that is independent of the community care assessment for the cared-for person and also encourages the use of direct payments for carers enabling them to purchase services.

The Carers (Equal Opportunities) Act, 2004 is additional legislation that goes on to offer carers improved choice with increased opportunities to lead a more fulfilling life. The government has recognized through legislation and guidance the importance of supporting people who are carers to lead lives outside of their caring role. This should allow carers to pursue other activities in order to maintain general health and well-being. Carers' assessments should be person-centred and should take account of their individual aspirations and the lifestyle choices of people. Meeting this aspect of support need will increase the carers' ability to continue offering support and care, thus enabling the cared-for person to continue living at home.

The Department of Health along with the Department of Education issued combined policy guidance (DOH, 2005) supporting carers' needs that suggests imaginative and flexible options that are required to best meet care needs. These options need not be aimed at taking away the direct caring responsibility for short breaks but could mean providing additional support for other duties that helps to free up their time. Help with shopping or household chores leaves more time for leisure or work activities away from the caring role. Each carer copes with the caring role in different ways. The assessor needs to listen carefully and develop and provide packages of care that are designed around individual needs, taking account of all the cultural and spiritual needs of the family carer.

It will be inevitable at some point that family carers will reach a point for a variety of reasons where they are no longer able to cope with the stresses of caring. People with learning disabilities often live with elderly parents who will also have their own support needs, for some this will cause people to move out of the family home into alternative care settings. At this point carers will need differing levels of support to come to terms with this major change in their role. This in itself can leave the carer dealing with feelings of guilt and loss that will require sensitive support and management. It is also worth noting that for parents who have supported their sons and daughters needs well into adult life, their caring role will rarely cease. It may decrease in terms of the time spent providing hands-on care, but family carers will continue to provide a vital role and will always be considered as carers maintaining their involvement where they feel it is appropriate. An example of this regards supporting health needs and access to health services, particularly when a person with learning disabilities requires hospital treatment. Carers are often available and will be willing and able to share crucial information to assist with treatment and support needs making hospital admission less traumatic for all. Carers will also be greatly concerned with standards of care and many will want to be involved with those providing care with a view to ensuring that needs are met adequately.

Partnership working with carers

In addition to direct care needs family carers can provide a valuable resource for developing and improving services. Family carer and user views can and should be used when evaluating services; in addition, involving family carers in staff training programmes can be beneficial. Staff teams benefit from greater understanding of family concerns and their experiences of using health services, and family carers can often provide a powerful message to mainstream service providers that will lead to improved services. Staff will also benefit from having a clear understanding of the unique experiences of families and how to improve communication and partnership between all the relevant parties. Davis (2005) developed a training resource to encourage carer involvement in staff development initiatives in learning disability teams. Similar approaches would benefit mainstream services to create greater awareness of the needs of people with learning disabilities and their carers. Lack of awareness is cited as one of the barriers faced when people with learning disabilities attempt to access health care with assumptions being made about what people need and what might be in their best interests. Any initiatives that are designed to assist with training and improving awareness must be welcomed.

Patient and Public Involvement Forums (PPI Forums) were set up in 2003 with a view to improving quality and standards in the NHS. The forum is made up of volunteers from the general public who have an interest in shaping and influencing the health services of the futures. Members are from differing groups who use health services, and people from all backgrounds are encouraged to join groups. One aspect of the role of the Patient and Public Involvement Forums is to seek views from users and to make recommendations that lead to service improvements. Carers and users who have direct experience of health care provision for people with learning disabilities involved in patient and public involvement forums will help to increase awareness of both the positive and negative experiences and lead to improved care.

Carers' health needs

For many carers the NHS will be the first and main source of contact with any services. The national strategy for carers, *Caring for Carers* (DOH, 1999a) made recommendations that primary care services, amongst other things, needed to identify their patients who were carers and offer them routine checks of their physical and emotional health (Keeley and Clarke, 2003). For those who choose to continue with their caring role these recommendations will help to ensure they are offered all the support required to meet their needs.

People who provide substantial levels of support are reported to seek primary care advice at increased levels because high levels of stress and anxiety associated with their caring role increase the potential for physical problems such as back pain (Arksey and Hirst, 2005). Incentives are now in place to encourage primary care teams to develop carer registers informing practices which patients are providing care to allow for additional health checks and support provision. Primary care teams need to respond appropriately, referring on to secondary care for additional support as necessary and informing these patients about entitlement to carer assessments. Maintaining the health and well being of carers is of significant importance enabling their caring role to continue.

Specialist care providers

Despite the overall majority of people residing with family carers there are substantial numbers of people who are reliant on teams of paid carers to support and/or provide for their everyday care needs. Across the country there are numerous establishments offering various types of accommodation. Many adults who have learning disabilities live relatively independent lives with minimal support needs, but others require support throughout the 24-hour period. Care is provided in a wide range of accommodation. The overwhelming majority of services provide social care and employ staff with differing skills and competencies. Staff teams are expected to give advice to the people with learning disabilities in their care as well as provide for all aspects of daily living. As with family carers they will at times take on an advocacy role, speaking out on behalf of the person when needed in conjunction with the people and their family carers as appropriate. The role carries great responsibility and with it the need to be skilled and observant in addressing preventative health measures and acting appropriately in order to ensure access to adequate health care in terms of maintaining mental and physical health and well-being.

Identifying ill health

Throughout this text reference is made to the problems faced by people with learning disabilities when accessing health services. Recognizing the need to seek advice from health services can prove problematic as staff teams providing care can often misinterpret clues with treatable health-related conditions going unnoticed. Carers, whether paid employees or family members, are in a position that allows enhanced knowledge of the person for whom they care. They will most likely hold information about the likes and dislikes of the person, will be best placed to recognize changes in moods and behaviour patterns and will, more often than not, be able to get the best response from the person. For people with severe learning disabilities who may have some difficulty conveying their own needs in the conventional way, the carer will be well placed to recognize potential for ill health and will need to respond accordingly, thus detecting and preventing illness.

It is completely unnecessary to tolerate poor health. Primary care teams give advice and support and should be used at the earliest opportunity. People with learning disabilities are often reliant on others to recognize that they are unwell and may need to visit a doctor, dentist, optician or any other clinician. The role of the carer will be to ensure access to the various and relevant health care providers. Anyone who has a caring role with people who have learning disability will have some level of responsibility for ensuring health needs are met. *Valuing People* (DOH, 2001c) sets targets for all people with learning disabilities to have a named health facilitator. The person best placed to fulfil this role at an individual level is the direct carer. Family carers ensure health needs are met for many people; for others the paid care staff who provide support on a daily basis will be best placed to take on the role. To fulfil this role adequately carers, both paid and unpaid, may require additional support and/or education in order to assist in both the prevention and detection of poor health. Professionals linked to the local learning disability teams are able to offer support in assessing and assisting to meet health needs.

Carers and individuals with learning disabilities can become unnecessarily tolerant of conditions connected to health, and lack awareness that treatments may be available that could offer either cure or help to alleviate the symptoms. Learning-disability teams or people employed in strategic health facilitation posts can develop and provide educational programmes to raise awareness on health related matters. This is explored in more detail in Chapter 3 of this text.

Preventing ill health

Carers providing support must be much more vigilant to improve health care standards. Family carers are able to provide a broad range of support, carrying out everyday tasks with few constraints. However, employed carers are often restrained by a number of rules and regulations that can create obstacles to meeting health needs.

Some tasks are not permitted in social care environments or will require a competent staff team. These tasks range from everyday personal care needs like cutting toenails to more invasive procedures such as monitoring blood sugar levels or administering emergency treatments for epilepsy. Family carers will often have developed these competencies for their loved ones over a period of time and will have little difficulty in providing for a range of care procedures.

Clearly constraints are required to minimize risks and ensure maintenance of health and safety. This, however, needs to be balanced with the risks of not undertaking these tasks when needed. Health and social care providers are faced with some additional challenges when balancing legislation and other rules that can sometimes be counter-productive, particularly when trying to encourage and empower people with learning disabilities to have greater independence and autonomy.

General observations and personal care support

When supporting people with learning disabilities there are a number of observations all those in a caring role can look out for and take action on where appropriate. All carers need to pay particular attention to aspects of self-care. Greater emphasis and attention to personal hygiene can help to prevent certain problems arising. Impacted earwax causing pain, discomfort and impaired hearing is often found during health screening. Once diagnosed as a problem the GP may recommend intermittent use of treatments like ear drops that can minimize this build-up of wax. Alternatively greater attention to detail when supporting someone with personal care needs may reduce reoccurrence. If this is a recurring problem, observation and early preventative action will reduce the effect on the person. Skin complaints are also quite common, for example, people with Down's syndrome can have dry and itchy skin conditions. Regular care with appropriate skin creams help to alleviate the effects of dry skin making the person more comfortable. Some key areas for carers to be extra vigilant in are listed in Table 6.1.

In addition to some of the routine daily concerns for health surveillance listed in Table 6.1 one must observe and take action where there are changes

Table 6.1 Personal hygiene and general care

Skin Care	Seek advice from GP and ensure treatments are given as advised.
Dental Care	Think about the support needs required to clean teeth. Offer support with regular visits to dentist. Monitor and advise on diet.
Foot Care	Make sure nails are cut and or filed regularly. Seek advice from podiatrist if needed.
Ears	Seek advice and ensure appropriate treatments are given.
Eyes	Seek advice and have regular vision checks with optician.
Diet	Ensure that people are offered and supported to eat a balanced diet along with accessible health promotional advice.

in patterns of behaviour, for example, A sudden increase in uncooperative or difficult behaviour patterns or changes in mood, such as lethargy or depression. Changes of this type are a cause for concern and carers should seek medical advice where appropriate. Differences in dietary habits and fluid intake may also indicate underlying medical problems. Some of these difficulties are discussed in Chapter 3. All carers will need to be more responsive to changes that could indicate medical causes. Table 6.2 lists questions and responses for all carers to consider with regard to monitoring health needs.

In health discussion with people with learning disabilities and their carers it is not uncommon to find that follow-up care can sometimes be intermittent. There are examples of repeat prescriptions being issued at the request of carers with no regular GP review with the person. In the study completed by Harrison, Plant and Berry (2004) one person had not seen the GP for 14 years yet continued to take prescribed psychoactive medication. In such cases the family carers and the GP will perhaps feel that this approach is possibly less traumatic and disruptive for all, however, continuing treatment of this type without seeing the patient

Table 6.2 Indications for medical care

Medical query	History	Action
Is the person in your care taking long-term medication?	→ If yes when was the medication last reviewed	→ Ask the prescribing Dr to review regularly
Do they require regular blood tests for diagnosed condition? e.g. Thyroid function, epilepsy or diabetes	→ If yes find out how often this will be required	→ Ask the Dr who treats the condition to review regularly
Are they eligible for national screening programmes? e.g. Breast and cervical screening	→ Check age. Breast – Women over 50; Cervical – Women 25–64	→ Arrange appointment with GP if no regular invites are issued
Do they have a history of high blood pressure?	→ If yes when was it last checked?	→ Ask for monitoring with practice nurse
Are there any age related changes e.g. menopause	→ If concerns are raised	→ Seek advice from relevant clinician

carries risks that are unacceptable and would not be tolerated in the majority of cases.

As we get older health-related problems increase and carers will need to be aware and look out for age-related problems. Many older people who have learning disabilities will not be offered support to have tests for failing eyesight. This is usually due to lack of awareness or thought regarding need on the part of those providing care. Having some knowledge of potential changes related to age and gender is important when supporting the needs of people with learning disabilities. There are numerous ailments that people can develop and this text does not attempt to cover them all, however, carers will need to provide for each eventuality and where concerns are raised with regard to any aspect of health need advice should be sought. Chapter 2 looks at different roles of members of the specialist team who can provide different levels of support, although the first and most appropriate contact will most likely be with the GP and other members of the primary care team.

Attendance at GP surgery or out-patient appointments

Visiting the GP surgery can be a stressful and anxious outing and taking steps to prepare for appointments will benefit all involved. Arriving unprepared with some uncertainty about why you are there will lead to frustrations for all. Doctors will need clear and concise factual information to enable them to reach a diagnosis or conclusion about what needs to happen next. They will inevitably need to ask a number of questions as part of the consultation process.

As the carer offering support you will need to ascertain and be clear about the level of input the person you are supporting will require. Asking yourself the questions in Text Box 11 and determining answers will help you to be prepared.

Text Box 11

Ask yourself these questions:

1. How much help will the person need to communicate?

    Can the person speak?

    What support will the person need from you?

2. What do I know about the presenting problem? ▶

3. What affect is it having on the individual?

4. What do I know about the person's health history?

5. How will the individual respond to environment/waiting rooms/times, etc? Might the person need a double appointment?

6. How might the individual respond to examination if required?

7. Will the person need help to understand what treatment is suggested?

8. Consider support needs in respect of consent to proposed treatments.

Clearly the person with learning disability needs to have involvement throughout this process prior to making appointments and during the appointments, bearing in mind that different people will require varied levels of support to answer questions and understand recommendations. Family carers will often remember relevant health history, but employed carers will need to take relevant health related information with them. In supporting people with this process it will also be useful to discuss and offer reassurance to the person involved, checking that they are happy and clear about what is planned.

The role of carers in improving health needs is of vital importance and cannot be underestimated. Making sure people have someone they trust and who knows them well and is well prepared will go some way to ensuring positive and improved outcomes are achieved.

Conclusion

Family carers are providing ongoing support to people with learning disabilities and as such will develop a range of support needs in their own right. Government legislation has been introduced that recognizes the vital efforts of carers and gives an entitlement to assessments of their own needs that allows for pursuit of personal goals with additional support from primary care teams monitoring of health needs.

This chapter has looked at carers and their needs and the role they have in supporting the cared-for person. It is recognized that large numbers of people who have learning disabilities will be residing with family carers often well into adulthood with parents continuing to provide for ongoing care and support. During this time carers will have developed a broad range of skills and in-depth knowledge regarding individual needs and knowledge of service provision that should be harnessed. Building partnerships and seeking support from carers in educational staff initiatives has been explored with greater emphasis placed on seeking and using views of family carers when evaluating and developing mainstream services.

Health care needs of people with learning disabilities and the role of carers including family and paid staff are explored with some practical guidance on what general observations should be made. Additional guidance and ideas that enable carers to gain the most from appointments with health care professionals is offered. It is also worth noting that many individual mainstream health professionals will have had minimal contact with someone who has learning disabilities and to achieve positive outcomes may require information and support from the carer.

Meeting the health needs of people with learning disabilities can be a complex and difficult task. It will require building of partnerships and relationships with people with learning disabilities, their carers and the relevant health professionals. Family carers as well as paid carers carry great responsibility for ensuring the health needs of people in their care are met. This role must be tempered with the need to ensure that people with learning disabilities have the opportunity to be given meaningful choices and are included in making their own health care decisions.

Meeting the health needs of people with learning disabilities in primary care settings

7

Introduction

Prevention and early detection of illness is important to everyone. Our first reaction to feeling unwell is to consider whether we would benefit from seeing the doctor. This poses difficulties for some people with learning disabilities who may often be reliant on others to recognize that they are unwell and may need to visit a doctor, dentist or optician, etc. For various reasons this can be overlooked. The focus in this chapter is to consider the provision of general medical services provided by the GP and other health professionals.

This chapter focuses on issues related to identification of people with learning disabilities and managing and monitoring their health needs in the primary care setting. Collaborative work between specialist teams and primary care services is explored as an option to identifying health needs and ensuring treatment plans are clear. There has been great debate recently in the learning disability arena regarding terminology and interpretation of definitions when developing registers. In practice experience has shown a reluctance to use what is seen as outdated terminology despite recommendations from the department of health. The chapter explores some of the terminology linked to coding systems used in primary care and also highlights the need for a consistent approach when identifying patients and allocating codes.

The *Valuing People* target (2001c) of offering all people health action plans is also discussed and concludes by offering some guidelines to assist with improving interactions and access to primary care services.

Identifying practice populations

An estimated 2% of the population are expected to have some form of learning disability. Health targets set in the White Paper, *Valuing People* (DOH, 2001c) stated that all people with a learning disability were to be registered with a GP and that general practices in partnership with specialist learning disability teams would be able to identify all people with a learning disability registered with the practice by 2004. These targets have proved difficult to achieve in some areas for a variety of reasons. Changes in the way general medical services are funded has created a new way of working in primary care with an emphasis on quality and outcomes. Difficulties arise when applying definitions of learning disability, as some uncertainty remains about who should and should not be included on a register of people with learning disabilities. The opening chapter discusses definitions in greater detail in an attempt to offer some clarity.

Primary care funding

Funding in primary care has gone through major change in recent years, with the implementation of the new general medical service contract (GMS) (DOH, 2002). General practices have had to develop a range of clinical registers necessary to monitor their patients and to gain payments. Although people with learning disabilities inevitably appear on registers linked to their medical condition, there was no actual requirement within the new general medical services contract to facilitate the development of registers for learning disabilities on its initial implementation in April 2004. This perpetuated a failure to see any benefits for practices, as there were no financial incentives for developing and maintaining a register of patients who had learning disabilities. In addition many GPs, when asked, have difficulty equating clinical need for registers or offering a proactive service despite evidence suggesting that inviting people for routine screening can identify a range of unmet health needs. From April 2006, almost two years after the *Valuing People* (DOH, 2001c) target for identifying the practice populations has passed, new additions to the contract and quality outcomes framework include developing a register of patients who have learning disabilities. This will bring about changes that will make GPs and the wider primary care team much more receptive to identifying their patients who have learning disabilities and developing a register of people.

Developing a register

When considering who should be included in a register it is perhaps useful for primary care teams to consider the benefits to individuals. At present the requirement is merely to keep a register of those people who have learning disabilities. Some primary care teams will be proactive in provision of care, perhaps through inviting those included on a register in for health checks, but others may not consider this level of service without further incentives or enhanced payments.

Setting up clinical registers in primary care is now commonplace as a requirement for the quality outcomes framework that is linked to payment. There are a number of codes used to identify people with a range of medical conditions. People with these medical conditions are relatively easy to find through the electronic records. A register of people with diabetes, for example, will be developed relatively easily through searching for diagnostic codes and for the prescribed drug treatments. Identification of someone with learning disabilities, however, is not so easy as there will inevitably be differences in treatment plans and diagnosis. In the case of someone with learning disabilities the description regarding a person's level of intellectual functioning on file can be varied or non-existent leaving it very difficult in some cases for primary care teams to be sure that allocating a code for learning disability is appropriate.

Evans *et al.* (2005) report problems with records summarization that relies on historical and descriptive information with individual judgements as to whether to include people or not. Terminology can be very ambiguous. Child health teams use descriptors like 'developmental delay', 'global delay' or 'learning difficulty' to describe children with wide ranging problems and who may or may not have a learning disability as defined within *Valuing People* (DOH, 2001c). A child who has dyslexia, for example, may not have impaired intellectual functioning but may be described on file as having a learning difficulty. This can present difficulties with the potential for some people being labelled incorrectly as having learning disabilities.

Much of the language used and accepted in the past to describe someone with learning disabilities appears outdated and at worst perpetuates the negative image of people. People from the older population may be described in their records as being 'mentally deficient', 'subnormal' or 'retarded'. All of this terminology creates problems for the mainstream health professional and others working within primary care, as unless they are knowledgeable about the individual and the variety of terms that have been used to describe this group, there may well be a continued reluctance to include people on a learning disability specific register.

Although different terminology presents problems and confusion with identification a bigger problem may involve convincing primary care of the benefits of developing this information. Whittaker (2004) suggested that applying labels to people may not always be to their benefit, however guidance issued by the Valuing People Support Team (2004) suggests that registers can be used to monitor the overall health status of people who have learning disabilities and will assist with monitoring numbers of people who access wider health services. In the long term this information will be of value in monitoring both improvements in health inequalities and access to services.

Use of READ codes

READ codes are used in primary care to help clinicians identify individuals and their specific health needs. There are numerous codes that are used to record diagnosis, treatments and to identify ongoing health needs. Clinical information systems and registers rely on codes allowing general practice to monitor numbers of patients with various conditions.

The system of coding within primary care is complex and this text is not intended to offer a comprehensive explanation of READ codes. Further information on this can be found through the web site for the National NHS Information Authority.

There has been much debate when developing primary care registers about terminology and what code should be used as an appropriate descriptor. Health facilitators along with colleagues in primary care are working through this with an expectation that guidance will be issued to support the development of registers from April 2006. One code that is favoured by some is a newly created code, 918e, is simply 'on learning disability register'. Other available codes have used used what was thought by many in Britain to be inappropriate language (see Table 7.1). This caused reluctance to code at all as the term 'mental retardation' was thought to be both outdated and derogatory. In many cases where codes have been used in primary care, gaining an accurate list that includes the right people has proved difficult, due to differing interpretations of the definitions given and the number of codes available.

A requirement to develop a register should lead to national uniformity. Using the same code will not clarify the problem of identifying those who may benefit from such measures; this will best be achieved through developing partnerships between specialist learning disability teams and primary care teams. Many primary care trusts have now taken on board recommendations from *Valuing People* (DOH, 2001c) and from further supporting guidance (Giraud-Saunders *et al.*, 2003). Several now have access to a lead professional who has knowledge of learning disabilities and is available to support primary care teams with identifying their practice populations with a view to improving overall access to health care services.

Valuing People (DOH, 2001c) also suggested that all people with a learning disability were to have or at least be offered a Health Action Plan by June 2005. Of course you would first need to be able to clearly identify this group to then offer this as a service to them. There are several complexities also involved in

Table 7.1 READ Codes commonly used in primary care to identity people with learning disability

Code	Heading
918e	On learning disability register
E3	Mental Retardation
EU7(X)	Mental Retardation
EU8IZ	Learning disability Nos
E2F	Specific Delay in development
13Z4E	Learning Difficulty
Pjyy4	Fragile X Syndrome
PJO	Down Syndrome

(NHS Information Authority 2005)

Table 7.2 Health action planning codes

Code	Heading
9HB3	Learning disabilities health assessment
9HB1	Learning disabilities health action plan offered
9HB0	Learning disabilities health action plan declined
9HB4	Learning disabilities health action plan completed
9HB2	Learning disabilities health action plan reviewed

(NHS Information Authority 2005)

monitoring who has a health action plan. Since the publication of *Valuing People* (DOH, 2001c) additions to READ codes have been introduced to enable monitoring of numbers of people who have had or been offered plans. These codes can be seen in Table 7.2. They are of benefit in measuring clinical outcomes for this group as well as monitoring the number of people who have plans.

Checklist for identification of learning disability

When summarizing electronic records in primary care there will be a number of things recorded on file that may suggest that a person has learning disabilities.

Medication and other treatments will be of very little value as no one treatment will be unique to people with learning disabilities. There may well be cues on file related to social and educational factors that will help clarify whether it is appropriate or not to include someone on a learning disability register. There are a number of questions to ask the health facilitator for learning disabilities or members of the specialist learning disability team.

Does the person have a clear diagnosis on file?

It may be clearly stated in the records that a person has learning disability or mental handicap. Alternatively the diagnosis may be linked to learning disability like Down's syndrome or Fragile X. Diagnoses of this type will indicate some level of learning disability that would suggest the need for inclusion on a register. It should be noted that the degree of disability arising from such diagnoses will vary immensely. However, it may be beneficial to the individuals to consider all who fall into this category for inclusion on a register as there will be a number of associated health problems linked to their genetic disorder.

Did or does the person attend special school?

It will be useful to find out from education or learning disability colleagues the specific names of schools in your local area and to distinguish between special schools for children with physical disability as opposed to schools catering for children who have learning disability. People who have attended schools for children who have severe learning disabilities or difficulties as defined within education will almost definitely fall into the category for inclusion on a register. Those attending moderate learning disability schools will have a high probability of benefiting from inclusion also. The type of education received may only be clear if there is correspondence on record either directly from the schools or from paediatric services. Health facilitators linking into specialist learning disability teams can also offer advice where there may be doubts.

Does the person live in a particular residential setting?

There may be a number of residential homes in the local area that will be registered to take people who have learning disabilities. The people living at such an address will have been assessed as having learning disabilities in order to gain a residential place or tenancy at the home. There will be various types of accommodation to meet the needs of people with learning disabilities in each area making it useful to liase with specialist learning disability teams to get the relevant information.

Does the person access the learning disability services?

If the person is receiving services from the learning disability team there should be correspondence on record indicating what services or which professional has worked with them. In these cases it will be fairly safe to say they have been assessed by a member of the team as having learning disabilities and are therefore eligible to access specialist support. All of these individuals could be included on a register of people with learning disabilities.

Exclusions

When summarizing notes there will inevitably be some individuals about whom it may not be clear as to whether they have learning disabilities or not. It may be useful to consider that some conditions are excluded unless also clearly coupled with an impaired intellectual functioning.

Some disorders may be referred to on file as 'learning difficulty' and in isolation would not constitute as having a learning disabilities as defined in *Valuing People* (DOH, 2001c). These could include people with some of the following: cerebral palsy or other physical disabilities, dyslexia, attention deficit hyperactivity disorders, behavioural and emotional difficulties and some people with autistic spectrum disorders, particularly those who have a high level of intellectual functioning. Although there may be a higher prevalence of all of these conditions amongst people who have learning disabilities, they are certainly not exclusive to the group. Before including people with these conditions it would be useful to determine their level of intellectual functioning and whether a diagnosis of learning disability is also present.

For further clarification it would also be unusual to find a person with learning disabilities who has attained average or above levels of academic achievements such as GCSEs or who attended mainstream education without additional support. Skills required to coordinate complex tasks such as learning to drive a vehicle or purchasing a house would not usually be apparent or expected in a person who has learning disabilities.

The above questions and exclusions are there to serve as a guide only. People with learning disabilities are individual and unique and need to be viewed as such. Their knowledge and skills will differ, which reiterates the difficulty and possibly the need of identifying all of the suggested 2% of the population.

Primary care teams who know their patients well will perhaps be able to make judgements on the benefits of including individuals on any register. If clinical need demands it and there are potential benefits to the person then they could perhaps be included. In addition and as a general rule, teams should use the resources available through access to specialist advice if there is any doubt about whether or not to include someone on a register.

Health needs assessment

Once the practice register is compiled, consideration about monitoring the health needs of those included on it is beneficial. There is evidence to suggest that health screening is beneficial to people with learning disabilities revealing unmet needs and creating opportunities for improved health (Barr et al., 1999, Cassidy et al., 2002). Although at present there are no apparent financial incentives for primary care offering annual or regular health screens that are over and above that offered to the general population, there are clear benefits to the individual. Detecting and monitoring conditions related to other clinical registers will bring financial rewards to primary care as well as contributing to improved health and well-being of the person involved.

There is much debate in the field of learning disability about health assessment and the development of health action plans and who is best placed to take a lead role. Collaborative work is required to ensure that people get the adequate range of advice and support to manage and improve their health. Many primary care trusts now have access to a lead professional or health facilitator for learning disabilities who can act as a catalyst for promoting the health needs of people who have learning disabilities and developing initiatives that encourage proactive approaches to health assessment.

Department of Health guidance (2002) suggests that primary care or mainstream health professionals will need to have some involvement in assessment and initiation of health action plans to ensure that appropriate advice is given. It should however be recognized that a shared approach to assessments is likely to bring the greatest benefit in many cases. The overall assessment should take account of a number of health issues that have been identified as particular relevance to people with learning disabilities. Valuing People (DOH, 2001c) listed these as oral and dental care, fitness and mobility, continence, vision, hearing, nutrition, emotional needs, medication and side effects and finally any records of screening. The above list reflects some common health issues that when left unchecked can create difficulties for people with learning disabilities. The list is not exhaustive and must take into account other aspects of health and lifestyle.

There are a number of assessment tools available to guide the process. Beange, et al. (1999) suggested 15 areas of health that would benefit from screening that are also easily treated or preventable conditions. The areas mirror those included in Valuing People (DOH, 2001c) with additions to include the treatment and prevention of chronic constipation, review of epilepsy treatments and regular screening for thyroid deficiency, particularly for patients who have Down's Syndrome. Further conditions included in Beange et al. (1999) that are common in people with learning disabilities and would benefit from checks and preventative measures are gastro-oesophageal disease and osteoporosis.

Health screening is being carried out in several areas of the country. Some are being conducted within primary care (Benson, 2004) others by members of the learning disability team (Pritchard, 2003). Both of these projects report similar findings with most people identified as having otherwise unknown but treatable conditions. In both models care treatments are prescribed as necessary although those people seen initially by learning disability services required follow-up appointments with the GP to gain some treatments. Benson (2004) reported that the GP involved in the study gained in confidence and had greater understanding of the health requirements of people with learning disabilities at the end of the project. The clinical knowledge of primary care professionals must not be underestimated and through collaborative protocols in developing assessment tools and templates linked to the electronic clinical systems used in primary care, all aspects of health can be considered. Identified heath issues require input from a range of professionals and the person who is supporting healthcare for someone who has learning disabilities will need to be sure that access to various professionals is encouraged.

A flexible approach to assessment will also benefit individuals. Some primary care teams along with health facilitators and/or learning disability nurses are conducting joint clinics with home visits offered for those who have difficulty getting to clinics. This approach ensures no one is excluded from health screening initiatives.

Health action plans

Following on from assessment of health needs comes a health action plan. Good Practice Guidance (DOH, 2002) suggests that plans need to be varied. All examples given in the Good Practice Guidance suggest that input from the primary care team will be needed in most if not all cases. In practice plans could be in the form of hand-held documents that also offer historic health information and enable people to keep all their appointments together. Other people will need a visual reminder of actions. Their plan may include photographs of people or places relevant to the actions required.

Health action plans are something many non-learning disabled people carry around mentally. We may tell ourselves that we need to eat a healthy diet, give up smoking, drink less alcohol, exercise more or visit the dentist – some of us will achieve some or all of these goals, some may not. Whichever category you fit it is unlikely, however, that you have this information on paper in written formats. This illustrates the importance of including the person with learning disabilities throughout the assessment process and in developing any actions arising from it. It would be fruitless to state as an action that people who are perhaps overweight need to change their diet or take up more exercise if they had no intention or the will to carry out this action. Alternatively that person may agree to attend some educational sessions regarding healthy eating to help raise awareness of the benefits of eating a healthy diet prior to them deciding to make any changes.

Health action plans may be in differing formats based on local needs however Department of Health guidance (DOH, 2002) suggests that all plans should be based on five key principles, the first is that the values of rights, choice, inclusion and independence are supported throughout the plan. Plans should be person-centred and take account of the individual's desires and wishes and their right to access all mainstream health services. Second, the health action planning process includes the need to develop strategic actions designed to support and develop the process. The third principle highlights the need to address individual as well societal influences of health. This includes health issues related to syndrome-specific needs, and cultural needs as well as those in relation to lifestyle and their social status. A fourth key principle is in relation to the shared responsibility. It is clear that no one organization or department can take responsibility for all aspects of health. A good health action plan may involve many stakeholders with the person with learning disabilities at the centre. Other players will be involved in ensuring specific actions are maintained, members of the primary care team including GPs and practice nurses will be expected to provide the main point of NHS contact. The fifth and final principle is that the process of health action planning is inclusive and supportive of the health initiatives designed to minimize and reduce health inequalities and improve access.

Making health action plans accessible

Developing person-centred health action plans can be time consuming and although input will be required from within primary care in deciding upon actions, it may not be possible under current time constraints for primary care teams to design plans in individualized accessible formats. Carers and members of the learning disability team will need to consider and facilitate this process. Some people with learning disabilities will be able to develop plans themselves, others will require support. Some examples of plans with brief case history are shown in the Detailed Good Practice Guidance (DOH, 2002).

Learning disability teams nationally will support people to develop individualized plans using photographs that can include images of the clinic or the appropriate health professional. These visual images help to involve and include the person to understand where, what and who may be involved in their health care.

A national group is currently underway looking at developing a care pathway to inform the process required to obtain a health action plan. It is hoped this will clarify the process and that it will offer additional guidance for the various professionals involved in the complexities of developing health action plans. Gaining greater clarity in how to get a plan and who needs to be involved will be of benefit to all involved.

Guidelines for accessible primary care services for people with learning disabilities

There are inevitable barriers to gaining access to health care settings much of which were discussed in Chapter 3. Primary care teams need to be instrumental in reducing health inequalities experienced by this group, however, they are likely to experience some difficulties when delivering care to a small number of people who have learning disabilities. The following tips are offered as suggested solutions to reducing some of the barriers.

Registers

Identify patients who may require greater support to access your service and develop a register so you know who your patients with learning disabilities are.

How do patients find their way around surgery?

Think about how patients with limited literacy skills will find their way around. You could work with advocacy services to gain ideas on improving the working environment. Photographs of the team and colour coding are all helpful to all patients. Consider the telephone or automated systems used to contact the surgery. Is it easy to follow with clear and concise instructions?

Planning consultations

For the small number of people with learning disabilities who will have difficulty waiting or fully communicating their needs, it may be beneficial to offer double appointments. You could also consider the benefit of offering first or last appointments to minimize disruption to the patient and others waiting. This will ensure time is allocated and used to greater effect. People with learning disabilities will benefit from having information explained using language they understand and from being given time to ensure that they can explain their problem and that they can understand the treatment plan they need to follow when they are at home.

Regular health checks

A proactive approach is advocated to help support people with learning disabilities recognize and identify their own health needs. You could consider holding a clinic for those identified on a register involving the GP and/or practice nurse. This could also involve a community learning disability nurse or health facilitator. Working together in this way will ensure that health action plans are offered and developed for people with learning disabilities. Martin, Axon and Baillie (2004) report on the success of a joint clinic held to undertake annual health checks for the people with learning disabilities held on their register.

Communicating with people

Always address people with learning disability first, including them in the consultation and only check out with a carer if something is unclear. Always involve the person with learning disability as much as possible. See additional information in Chapter 5.

Carer support

For people who require support from carers it may be helpful to request a consistent approach. For people with learning disabilities living in residential homes a carer who knows the person well will be best equipped to support the person and to share information regarding health needs if required. Those living with family carers will usually be supported by them.

Information leaflets

Having information available in formats people can understand will be beneficial. There are, for example, several health promotional leaflets about smoking, breast examination, cervical smears and dietary advice that are specifically designed for people with learning disabilities. The specialist learning disabilities team or the health facilitator can help you access these.

Consent and capacity

Think about patients' capacity to consent to any proposed intervention. Respect their decision, however, where there is doubt about capacity and consent utilize good practice guidance on consent and consider best interests as stated in the Mental Capacity Act (2005).

Referrals to other health professionals

When referring on to another health professional make sure your colleagues are aware that the person has learning disabilities and may need additional support and time during any consultations.

The guidelines above offer some guidance for health care professionals to consider when working with people who have learning disabilities. It is difficult to generalize and accurately categorize this group of people as each and every one of them will have their own individualized needs. The points above can be used to guide services in developing a flexible approach to meet the required needs of those individual patients. In many cases GPs and practice nurses along with other staff in primary care will be familiar with their patients and will be offering services to meet their needs. In addition, support can be found through accessing a whole range of services in health and social care as well as through voluntary agencies. Finding out what services are available in your own locality will prove beneficial.

Conclusion

Primary care services, in particular those provided through the GP, is more often than not the route into all other health services and will be the one service all members of society will access at some time in their lives. It is important that all members of the population have good access and responses to appropriate health care when required. Throughout this text health inequalities have been explored in relation to people with learning disabilities with the need to take a more proactive approach to both identifying and meeting their health care needs.

This chapter has focused particularly on services delivered by the GP and other practice staff and has explored opportunities to create comprehensive registers of those people who have learning disabilities. A checklist of items to assist with identifying the practice population is offered and can be used with assistance from colleagues from the specialist teams. In addition to this the health needs assessment linked to electronic templates has been highlighted.

Working collaboratively to not only ensure that people with learning disabilities are identified but are then also offered health screening and the opportunity to have a health action plan is a way forward. The chapter concludes by offering some guidelines that can be considered when offering consultation and services to people with learning disabilities.

There is from April 2006 a requirement carrying incentives for general practice to develop registers through additions to the general medical services contract (NHS Employers, 2006), it is hoped and encouraged that health screening and greater support for developing health action plans will follow as further incentives to improve the health status of people with learning disabilities. Working with local teams including health facilitators to gather evidence of health needs and to monitor health gains will be invaluable in the drive for continued health improvements.

Caring for people with learning disabilities in acute hospital settings

8

Introduction

Redesigning and transforming health services around the needs of individual patients is the basis for reforms set out in the NHS Plan (DOH, 2000). In this there is a commitment to develop a responsive service that must challenge discriminatory practice on the grounds of age, gender, disability, ethnicity, religion and sexuality. Despite this commitment there are continued concerns with regard to acute hospital services fully meeting the needs of people with varying vulnerabilities within current resources.

People with learning disabilities have varied experiences when accessing acute hospital services. Much of the research indicates a lack of awareness on behalf of mainstream health professionals of this group's needs in particular. Lack of awareness can lead to dissatisfaction and inappropriate responses to care needs. Research also indicates that people with all types of disability experience services that often fail to respond fully to their specialist needs (Atkinson and Scarloff, 1987; Keywood Fovarge and Flynn, 1999; Davis and Marsden, 2001). Being unaware presents particular difficulties when offering training, as Davis and Marsden (2001) point out that staff, when asked, stated that they felt they were adequately meeting the needs of patients who had disabilities. If this is the case, staff teams will fail to see the need to attend any awareness sessions related to this topic. This chapter seeks to highlight the need for greater awareness amongst mainstream hospital teams and offers some guidance that can lead to improving interactions with people who have learning disabilities and other vulnerable groups when accessing hospital services. The chapter looks at practical solutions for sharing and gathering information and suggests the need for collaborative work between mainstream secondary care teams, family carers and specialist learning disability teams.

Access to hospital services

Hospital teams offering acute care have the difficult job of needing to cater for the needs of several groups of people of all ages. Many fall into groups that perhaps are regarded as vulnerable and for a variety of reasons will have additional support needs. Recent reports into the care of older people within the acute hospital setting gives rise for concern particularly when ensuring their nutritional needs as well as their self care needs are adequately met and supported. A number of concerning issues were raised in the media and highlighted by a BBC panorama programme in 2005. Reports on food and drink being left out of reach with little attempt in some cases to offer support at meal times to those who needed it mirror those detailed by Glasby (2002) when reporting specifically on acute hospital care for people with learning disabilities. This shows that there is a need for teams to be much more aware and responsive to the individual needs of all patients and that difficulties with gaining access to high quality care is not unique to people with learning disabilities.

Accessing large general hospitals can be a frightening and daunting prospect for people. First, access to secondary care services is often required as a result of illness or injury, which, by its very nature, will give rise to some anxiety. Second, the inevitable investigative process that leads to diagnosis and treatment will more often than not create concern and stress for the individuals involved as well as their loved ones. Levels of anxiety depend upon the nature and severity of presenting symptoms as well as the individual involved. Health care staff need a level of awareness of the differing needs of all people to enable them to offer the most effective and individualized approach to care. For people with learning disabilities these levels of anxiety are heightened as a result of the difficulties they may have in understanding and adjusting to their surroundings.

Disability awareness

Levels of dissatisfaction between people with learning disabilities and their carers using hospital services have been widely reported (DOH, 1999b; Mencap 2004). Atkinson and Scarloff (1987) reported that nurses have a general lack of awareness of the special needs of disabled people. This theme is further picked up in research papers written since that time. In a study undertaken by Davis and Marsden (2001) nurses in the acute hospital felt there was not a problem in caring for those who have disability and in many respects the ward staff indicated that they managed the needs of people with disabilities effectively. However, the observations made during that study reported that practice was, at times, inappropriate. Problems highlighted were often due to staff shortages or possibly due to a lack of awareness and understanding of the varied needs of people with disabilities. The notion that one is dealing with issues effectively when many patients with disability report their dissatisfaction clearly indicates a lack of awareness of the real and varied needs.

Atkinson and Scarloff reported in 1987 that when admitted to hospital people with disabilities were also more likely to experience difficulties in communicating their needs to the nursing staff. This created difficulties when attempting to form positive and effective relationships between the health professional and the person with disabilities. Reports by Davis and Marsden (2001) and Glasby (2002) indicate that these difficulties continue. Reasons for this could be that staff teams are unfamiliar with the method of communication or possibly have a pre-conceived view of the person with disability. In this situation the health professionals need to use all their communication skills to help alleviate any problem and must always make attempts to communicate using methods people understand. Chapter 5 offers some guidance to assist health professionals with improved communication with people who have difficulty vocalizing.

Glasby (2002) discusses the variable nature of care given in hospitals and suggests that staff teams do not adequately use information gathered on admission to support the ongoing care needs of individuals. Other factors related to care needs are sometimes contradictory, for example, people with learning disabilities are often excluded from the health care decision making process on the grounds that they are unable to understand the issues and complexities involved (Keywood et al., 1999). In contrast to this Band (1998) found that hospital teams also make assumptions that people with learning disabilities are more able and proficient, particularly in providing for their own self care needs, than is actually the case. This again highlights the difficulties staff teams have in communicating with people with learning disabilities and gaining a clearer understanding of their needs. It is possible that teams are subconsciously taking what appears to be the easier option for the team or department without fully understanding the needs and potential consequences of their actions. Excluding people from some aspects of their care and decision making process can be disabling, but having greater expectations of the level of ability of people with learning disabilities can place them at risk. Publications that allude to this issue detail numerous cases that are mirrored nationally (Glasby, 2002; Mencap, 2004).

Cases from experience show that incorrect assumptions lead to people not being given adequate levels of support to ensure that even their basic needs are met. Food and drink are not taken simply due to a lack of support being given and reports of medication being left by the bedside to be knocked over or just not taken because the individual lacks skills and co-ordination to fulfil these tasks without support. Examples such as these reinforce the need for carers who feel compelled to stay at the hospital to provide ongoing support, and to ensure that these basic needs are met. Because carers step in to take care of patients, the health care teams fail to improve their awareness and make improvements in required knowledge and skills. The reliance on carers is also due to the lack of resources available, particularly in terms of staff – patient ratios. Davis and Marsden (2001) raise this issue and suggest that the environment in the hospital is unsuitable and can contribute to poor service in acute care. Inappropriate staffing levels are often the key factor in deciding whether individuals who have learning disability are put forward for surgery or any other invasive treatments. Any pre-operative plan must take account of the staff – patient ratio. Where necessary additional support should be found, particularly if this is all that is required to ensure successful treatment and recovery. Decisions such as these where there is limited knowledge of clients and their abilities require further debate, perhaps in a multi-disciplinary meeting that involves client and his or her carer to reach an agreed consensus and plan of action.

It must be acknowledged that for some people with complex needs there may be a real requirement for additional support. Consideration must also be given to who is best placed to provide that support. Some people with learning disabilities may find the hospital easier to cope with if they have familiar people around. For planned admissions it may be beneficial to all concerned for pre-admission visits to take place; this can help familiarize the person with members of the staff team and the environment. This can also help to alleviate any concerns on behalf of the staff team. Asking carers to make themselves available at crucial points in the treatment phase can also prove beneficial, for example, following a surgical procedure, during recovery from anaesthesia, it could be extremely beneficial to see a familiar face. It may be much easier for a parent to dissuade their son or daughter from removing dressings, catheters or other vital treatments at this crucial time in the early stage of recovery. Alternatively a paid carer, professional or advocate might be the best person to provide this level of support. Planning can be helpful to all involved. It will also ensure that the most appropriate carers are able to be there and involved without them feeling compelled to spend several hours at the hospital just in case they are needed.

Many of the difficulties regarding acute hospital care are from the direct experiences of people with learning disabilities, their carers and professionals working in the speciality. The knowledge and expertise of mainstream staff in delivering the clinical care as required to a wide range of people is not to be underestimated. Using clinical skills whilst also responding to the individual needs of all patients on a ward can be a complex task. This is coupled with the drive to improve discharge rates and reduce waiting times within the NHS. As Keywood and Flynn (2003) point out, it is hardly surprising that in this climate conflicts are created when managing someone in acute hospital settings who has additional needs that require extra time and sometimes complex care planning involving a number of external agencies.

Specialist liaison nursing services

Throughout this text reference has been made to the need for raising awareness, in particular around the needs of vulnerable adults in need of additional support. People with learning disabilities and other vulnerable patients may not easily fit the normally expected recovery times. Keywood et al. (1999) confirm the importance for additional time and staffing to be allowed for the achievement of successful outcomes. Achieving this on the first admission will also ensure that the need for readmission is far less likely.

There are a number of initiatives involving the appointment of a professional who takes lead responsibility for sharing information and developing policy and practice in an attempt to address the difficulties highlighted. Davis and Marsden (2001) discuss the benefits of the role of a clinical nurse specialist appointed to support the needs of all groups of people with disabilities through providing education to staff teams and offering reassurance to people with disabilities prior and during admission.

Services to specifically meet the needs of people with learning disabilities during hospital admission have also been reported. Glasby (2002) reports on the project that involved a small team of nurses and care staff with experience in learning disabilities who were appointed to not only support the educational needs of the hospital teams but to offer support, guidance and advice to people with learning disabilities and their carers. Their role involved offering support to eight acute hospitals and to several patients with learning disabilities from the point of referral to admission and discharge. The team were able to meet with the patient prior to admission and arrange a visit to the ward. In addition they offered support to the patient and ward staff while in hospital and made follow-up visits after discharge. This level of support ensures not only a successful outcome for the patient but offers support to family carers at an incredibly stressful time. It also gives clear recognition to the varied skills and ability of the staff team involved. Members of the liaison team with knowledge and expertise in working with people who have learning disabilities use their skills to good effect allowing the ward staff to offer the appropriate range of clinical skills required to support post-operatively.

Roles such as those are being developed in acute hospitals and improvements in care are noted. These posts have been developed in response to the various government documents offering good practice guidance. *Signposts for Success* (DOH, 1998) made a number of recommendations that could be easily addressed through the liaison nurse role, most notably ensuring that equal access to services is available by having an educational and advisory role. Developing and strengthening partnerships between mainstream and specialist service providers requires a level of understanding and respect for the varied roles. Working together to provide care and enhance each other's skills can only be of benefit to people with learning disabilities as well as those with all types of disabilities.

Some areas will have access to a specialist nurse working within hospitals but many will not. However, all areas will have a community learning disability team. Many of these teams will operate an open referral policy and will be available for advice. Since the publication of *Valuing People* (DOH, 2001c) health facilitators have also been appointed in some districts to work at a strategic level with the primary care trusts. Though their main focus will be developing primary care services, many of these facilitators are also available and regularly offer support and advice to hospital teams.

Sharing information

Personal health records were recommended in *Signposts for Success* (DOH, 1998) and there are a several examples of these available. Strategic health facilitators in Gloucestershire have developed a number of useful leaflets and information that is available on various pages of the Valuing People support team web site (2005). Recognizing the busy environment in hospitals and the difficulty staff teams have in finding time to consider lengthy case histories, the health facilitation team in Gloucestershire developed a traffic light assessment tool (Figure 8.1). This is completed by or with the person with learning disabilities prior to admission, and can be done with help from family or employed carers if needed. The tool is in three parts, red, amber and green. The red sheet contains information that is of crucial importance on admission and that all hospital team members dealing with the person need to know. It details current medication and offers a brief medical history along with a space for details regarding potential ability for consent. Information contained in the amber sheet is of greater importance for longer stays and should be used to refer to during the stay in hospital. Information is given regarding methods of communication of vital importance for ensuring that individuals are included and involved in all levels of their care. Greater detail is also included regarding support needs including the level of assistance an individual may need for aspects of self care. If these instructions are followed, basic needs should be understood and met. The green sheet offers more detailed information about likes and dislikes, any special routines and activities that may help the person to stay content while in hospital. This is additional information that could prove beneficial to all involved, could help ward teams have greater insight into some of the individual's behaviours and mannerisms and could include advice on how to respond to particular behaviours and idiosyncrasies. Anecdotal evidence from carers raises some concerns that staff teams often fail to respond to information related to certain idiosyncrasies. One parent had informed staff team on more than one occasion that their son, who had severe learning disabilities along with autistic tendencies, would not take fluids unless his drink was given in a particular cup yet staff on the ward failed to take this information seriously despite the young man repeatedly refusing drinks. Using the documentation shown in Figure 8.1 should help to alleviate this situation and ensure that staff teams have access to concise but important information regarding care needs.

This tool is just one of a number of useful formats currently being used across the UK in an attempt to improve information sharing. It recognizes the need for preparation, before, during and after admission and its use promotes the need for partnership working between mainstream staff teams who have the medical and surgical skills and specialist learning disability teams with skills to support the patients and their carers to understand and manage their health in a variety of settings. Ward staff need to be fully prepared and willing to use the information contained in the document and then act on it for successful outcomes to be achieved.

Gloucestershire Partnership **NHS**
NHS Trust

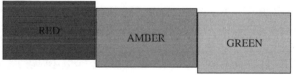

HOSPITAL ASSESSMENT
For people with learning disabilities.

> This assessment gives hospital staff important information about you.
> Please take it with you if you have to go into hospital.
> Ask the hospital staff to hang it on the end of your bed.
> Please note: Value judgements about quality of life must be made in consultation with you, your family, carers and other professionals.
> This includes Resuscitation Status.
> Make sure that all the nurses who look after you read this assessment.

Figure 8.1 Traffic light assessment tool

RED-ALERT

Things you <u>must</u> know about me

Name -
Likes to be known as -
Address -

NHS number -

Tel no-

Date of Birth -

GP -   Address:

Next of Kin -   relationship -   Tel no -
Key worker/main carer -   relationship -   Tel no -
Professionals involved -   Tel no -
Religion -   Religious requests -

Allergies –

Current medication –

Current medical conditions –

Brief medical history –

Level of comprehension/ capacity to consent –

Medical Interventions – how to take my blood, give injections, take temperature, medication, BP etc.

Behaviours that may be challenging or cause risk -

Heart (heart problems) –

Breathing (respiratory problems) -

Eating & Drinking issues -

Figure 8.1   (Continued)

AMBER	Things that are really important to me
Communication - How to communicate with me.	
Information sharing - How to help me understand things.	
Seeing/hearing - Problems with sight or hearing	
Eating (swallowing) - Food cut up, choking, help with feeding.	
Drinking (swallowing) - Small amounts, choking	
Going to toilet - Continence aids, help to get to toilet.	
Moving around - Posture in bed, walking aids.	
Taking medication - Crushed tablets, injections, syrup	
Pain - How you know I am in pain	
Sleeping - Sleep pattern, sleep routine	
Keeping safe - Bed rails, controlling behaviour, absconding	
Personal care - Dressing, washing etc.	
Level of support - Who needs to stay and how often.	

Figure 8.1 (Continued)

GREEN			
Things I would like to happen		**Likes/dislikes**	
THINGS I LIKE Please do this:	☺	THINGS I DON'T LIKE Don't do this:	☹
Think about – what upsets you, what makes you happy, things you like to do i.e. watching TV, reading, music. How you want people to talk to you (don't shout). Food likes, dislikes, physical touch/restraint, special needs, routines, things that keep you safe.			

Reproduced with permission from Gloucestershire Partnership NHS Trust
(Elliott and Dean 2004)

Figure 8.1 (Continued)

Planning for discharge

It may be useful to consider the effect that any illness, injury or treatment can have on a person with learning disabilities. Even following minor procedures the person with learning disabilities may have problems following the expected treatment plan. More people with learning disabilities are being supported to live independent lives and when fit and well will require minimal support, however minor ailments can present major difficulties with increased support needs. In these cases a full review of their care needs on discharge may be necessary. Consideration of appropriateness of the accommodation and standard recovery times may need to be reconsidered. Carers needs will also be a factor when planning discharge – will carers need additional help or aids and adaptations prior to discharge?

Many of these problems must be considered before or as near to admission as practical. If this has been done smooth transition between services will be likely. If not you may find the person or carer lacks the necessary skills to provide for aftercare. This could lead to either prolonged hospital stays, blocking vital beds or, if discharged too soon, create the need for readmission. Trying to resolve disagreements about the appropriateness of discharge after treatment can be a lengthy process, planning for potential support needs prior to discharge should help to avoid this.

Nationally there are some examples of intermediate care services that can offer additional support during discharge and recovery or the provision of nursing care beds to alleviate the need for long stays in an acute hospital bed. The key message is to consider needs on discharge as early in the process as is practical and familiarize yourself with your local learning disability service, which may be able to offer advice and/or practical support.

What steps can be taken to improve care?

Hospital departments are incredibly busy places. They are often under-resourced and anyone entering this environment who requires a high level of support could experience difficulties with the care provision if staffing levels are not reviewed. Some of the guidance that follows may appear time consuming, but they are points worthy of consideration and may assist in achieving positive outcomes. Careful planning will not only be effective for the person with learning disabilities but could also prove beneficial to all other patients.

There are a number of resources available offering advice or protocols that are useful when providing services to people with complex needs, in particular Royal National Institute of the Blind (2000) offers guidance for minimizing problems with eye surgery for people with severe learning disabilities. Lothian University Hospitals trust with Lothian Primary Care Trust (2002) offers an approach to collaborative working involving a liaison nurse post. Recognizing that not all hospitals have access to a specialist liaison nurse post, the guidance offered here could be beneficial when applied in a variety of situations. The varied nature of admissions is also considered with guidance offered on dealing with both planned and emergency admissions.

Planned admission

- Be prepared. Having a clearly identified and recorded plan of support needs will increase the chances of a successful outcome of any surgical procedure. This is of particular importance for people with severe learning disabilities who will be dependent on having a high level of support throughout their hospital stay.

- Gather as much information prior to admission to ascertain potential support needs and contact the learning disability team for further advice if required. Learning disability team members will be well advised to offer this information for anyone with whom they will be working.

- Ask for information in any hand-held record to be available. You could also be clear about the information that will be needed on admission so that the patient and carers can be prepared.

- Pre-operative visits to the prospective ward are advisable. This allows hospital staff to become familiar with an individual and helps to familiarize the person who has learning disabilities to the environment and the staff team. Members of the learning disability team or care providers could help with this.

- Consider length of stay required for people with learning disabilities and how to provide appropriate support during and after. Depending on the proposed treatment it may be possible to negotiate treatment for individuals as a day-patient. This depends on the ability of carers and the primary care team in providing aftercare. If a person with learning disabilities is likely to be less distressed and more easily 'managed' as an outpatient, then consultants may decide that the benefits may outweigh the risks.

- Don't be too rigid with discharge plans. Some people with learning disabilities may benefit from shorter or longer stays to ensure good recovery.

- When a person with learning disabilities needs support to access services, continuity is important. Where possible it will be beneficial if the same family carer or support worker escorts the patient on every visit. Hospital teams would be well advised to make this request of those providing care to the person.

- If the person with learning disabilities agrees, the main carer should be invited to accompany the patient on the day of admission and to take part in the admission process. It should be made clear that the admission process may be lengthy and a time commitment is required. Ask the person with learning disabilities or the carer to bring along any information regarding current care plan and medication.

Emergency admission

It is recognized that the ability to respond in a timely fashion will be dependent on priorities at the time of admission. Accident and emergency departments clearly have a need to prioritize the order they see patients based on clinical needs and should have clear guidelines that support this.

- Identify a main carer and make contact as soon as possible if one is not in attendance. This contact should take place as early as possible in the patient's admission to the accident and emergency department or other unit.
- Once it is established that the person has learning disabilities contact could be made with the local learning disability team who may be able to offer advice or, if appropriate, visit the department to assist with assessment and communication.
- If the person is to be transferred to another department the named nurse in the accident and emergency department should advise the nurse in charge of the receiving ward and provide an initial assessment of the patient's care needs.
- The person will require reassurance and will need to be introduced to the new environment, including the staff team and other patients.

All admissions

- A full assessment of the patient's needs should be undertaken, taking care to gain clarity on their everyday support needs, this will ensure all staff are aware of the level of support required for self care. Make sure that information taken from carers when appropriate is used and shared with the ward team.
- When considering treatments seek advice from the learning disability team, particularly if consent and capacity presents difficulties. Members of the learning disability team could help to ensure that consent information from a fully informed basis is offered to the patient.
- Family carers and staff members who know the individual well can offer constructive support and advice that ensures any procedures that are required are undertaken with maximum cooperation from the person with learning disabilities.

- Particular note should be made of the patient's medication regime, including the form of the preparation, times and methods of administration that may have been tailored very specifically to the individual patient.

- Doctors and nurses must try to explain procedures and treatment in a clear, straightforward way, which the individual understands. Care staff or family carers who know the person with learning disabilities well can help to interpret this information ensuring that they have understood all explanations.

- Find out from care staff and family carers what the person with learning disabilities was usually like before they became ill. It is important to gain as much information about the skills and abilities of the person when they are well as this will alleviate incorrect assumptions undue expectations.

- Where surgical procedures are required it may be beneficial to consider where the person with learning disabilities should be on the day's list. Allowing them to be first could benefit the unit and other patients waiting while minimizing distress and uncertainty for the person also.

- Arrange for a carer or someone the person knows to be available following any surgery, so a familiar person is available when he/she is in recovery.

- Make sure you have a plan of action for the whole in-patient period recorded in the person's medical records and ensure all relevant staff are made aware of it. This should include individual support needs of the person with learning disabilities and any changes to the standard staffing ratios.

- Adequate staff cover may be the most important consideration particularly if the person is being offered surgery or requires complex treatment plans. Pre-operative planning should involve carers and the learning disability team where appropriate who can advise and may be available to support the person at the most crucial stages of their a hospital stay.

- Always ensure that you include the patient in all conversations and consultations, be aware of your language, keeping it clear and concise using words the person understands. Allow time for the patient to ask you questions to ensure clarity.

- Consider pain relief. People with learning disabilities may not ask, but this does not mean they will not require it. Appropriate pain assessment techniques should be implemented to ensure adequate pain management. Seek advice from a pain specialist if in doubt.

- Never ask for a family carer or other support worker to give consent on behalf of an adult with a learning disability. Chapter 4 deals with issues related to consent and capacity.

- Where there are concerns regarding capacity you must consider best interests and if possible arrange to discuss treatment and care options with other clinicians and those closest to the person including family carers.

- Discharge planning should be discussed with the patient and the main carer at the time of admission, wherever possible. This will help to avoid misunderstandings and allow for forward planning where needed.

- The hospital staff could alert the community learning disability team to ensure a coordinated approach is planned prior to discharge.

Conclusion

For most of us being in hospital will be an alien experience. Despite this many of us will be able to rationalize the benefits and reasons for the need to be there. For many people who have learning disabilities this will be very different. The support required in understanding why they are there and why certain treatments are required will be much greater than for non-learning disabled patients. This presents challenges for teams working in busy hospital departments driven by targets designed to speed up discharge rates and reduce waiting times.

There are examples of initiatives involving working in partnerships with specialist teams or nurses that have been developed to assist with improving access to the most appropriate care for this group. To date the evidence presented shows clear improvements in clinical outcomes and in patient satisfaction where these initiatives are in place (Davis and Marsden, 2001; Glasby, 2002).

A general lack of awareness of needs leading to inadequate responses to care delivery features in much of the documented research. This chapter has highlighted this fact and has presented some examples of good practice along with guidance for improving the planning of admission and discharge where possible. This can involve making greater links with colleagues in specialist learning disability teams and improving on gathering all the relevant information about skills and abilities of the person with learning disabilities. Improving links with different professional groups assists with raising awareness of issues faced by all. Greater awareness brings with it the need to liase with each other and to seek the help and advice needed to improve care. *Valuing People* (DOH, 2001c) alluded to problems arising due to specialist teams taking an all-encompassing approach to care rather than seeking support from mainstream health services. It remains clear that both specialist learning disability teams and mainstream health teams need to work in partnership to ensure equal access to health care improves and moves us nearer to closing the health inequality gap.

Useful resources and web addresses

When working with people with learning disabilities there are a number of resources that are now, through access to the internet, easily found. The following list includes some of the key websites that include a wealth of information to help all staff, including mainstream health professionals, when developing initiatives that can improve the health experience of people with learning disabilities.

www.valuingpeople.gov.uk/index.htm
The valuing people support team was set up to support the implementation of the changes and recommendations set out in the White Paper, *Valuing People; A new strategy for learning disability for the 21st century*. The website contains a wealth of information with links to several important and useful documents including accessible leaflets.

www.valuingpeople.gov.uk/HealthPrimary.htm
This web page includes information and resources that will help when developing primary care services for people with learning disabilities.

www.valuingpeople.gov.uk/HealthHospital.htm
This page gives information on a range of people and resources that can help improve hospital services. It includes a hospital communication book and the traffic light tool in Figure 8.1.

www.npsa.nhs.uk/site/media/documents/1027_learningdisabilities_issues.pdf
The National Patient Safety Agency have compiled a report that looks specifically at understanding the patient safety issues for people with learning disabilities and offers recommendations around access to acute hospital services.

www.rcpsych.ac.uk/PUBLICATIONS/bbw/indcx.htm
The books beyond words series provide a very useful resource that can be used to prompt discussion with people with learning disabilities about a range of health related matters.
    Book Sales, Royal College of Psychiatrists, 17 Belgrave Square, London SW1X 8PG Tel: 020 7235 2351

www.changepeople.co.uk
The CHANGE picture bank contains a collection of drawings devised and developed with and by people with learning disabilities that are used to enhance written communications making them more accessible to people who have difficulty reading written information. CHANGE also offers a variety of publications aimed at people with learning disabilities.

Change publications, Unity Business Centre, Units 19 & 20 26, Roundhay Road, Leeds L57 1AB.

www.bild.org.uk
BILD is an organization dedicated to improving the lives of people with learning disabilities and provides a wealth of useful resources.

British Institute for Learning Disability, Campion House, Green Street, Kidderminster, Worcestershire, DY10 1JL Tel: 01562 723 010

www.elfrida.com
The Elfida Society offers a number of accessible leaflets and resources related to supporting health needs.

Elfrida Society, Tom Blyth Centre, 34 Islington Park Street, London N1 1PX Tel: 020 7359 7443

www.shropshirepct.nhs.uk/
The team in Shropshire have developed several accessible leaflets related to health that are accessible on their website under the heading learning disabilities.

www.downs-syndrome.org.uk
The Down's Syndrome Association, Langdon Down Centre, 2A Langdon Park, Teddington, TW11 9PS Tel: 0845 230 0372

www.dsscotland.org.uk
Down's Syndrome Scotland, 158/160 Balgreen Road, Edinburgh, EH11 3AU Tel 0131 313 4225

You will find detailed information about people with Down's Syndrome and their health needs. Both Down's Syndrome Scotland and the Down's Syndrome Association include health related information as well as additional information to support the ongoing needs of people who have down's syndrome.

www.learningdisabilities.org.uk
The Foundation for People with Learning Disabilities is involved in raising awareness of issues related to people who have learning disabilities and offers a wide range

of information to support professionals. The Foundation for People with Learning Disabilities, 83 Victoria Street, London, SW1H OHW
Tel: 020 7802 0300

www.fairadvice.org.uk/booklets.htm
Fairadvice offers a range of useful leaflets and CD roms to assist with raising awareness of health needs.
   FAIR 25–27 West Nicoloson Street, Edinburgh, EH8 9DB

www.rnib.org.uk
RNIB, UK National Customer Service, Bakewell Road, Orton Southgate, Peterborough, PE2 6XU

www.cancerscreening.nhs.uk
Good Practice in Breast and Cervical Screening for Woman with Learning Disability are found at this website.
   Cancer Screening Programmes, The Manor House, 260 Ecclesall Road South, Sheffield S11 9PS

www.mencap.org.uk
MENCAP provides support and information in all aspects of learning disability. Mencap City Foundation, 14 Porcupine Close, London, SE9 3AE

www.supported-living.org/
This web site has details of The MAP and PATH templates that are designed to support the development of person centred plans.

Links to health screening assessments and health record booklets

Health trusts and other organizations have developed a number of tools to aid in making health assessments and creating hand-held records. The following list offers a selection of these that can be found through the website links and is not intended in any way to promote one format over another. It is offered merely in an attempt to share some examples. It is possible that your local learning disability team have developed formats that are used in your own area.

www.dsscotland.org.uk/publications/learning-disability/keeping-well.pdf

www.downs-syndrome.org.uk/DSA IstLiterature.aspx#c6

www.fairfieldpublications.co.uk/okhealth.htm

www.lons.org/ahcp/grants2004/HealthBook.pdf

www.intellectualdisability.info/leaflets/health_check.pdf

www.mencap.org.uk/download/you_and_your_health.pdf

www.wales.nhs.uk/sites/documents/368/Welsh%20health%20check.doc

References

Abudarham, S. and Hurd, A. (eds) (2002) *Management of Communication Needs in People with Learning Disability*. Whurr, London.

Adults with Incapacity (Scotland) Act (2000) Scottish Executive. Edinburgh.

Albrecht, G. and Devlieger, P. (1999) The disability paradox, in *Difficult Decisions: Social and Ethical Implications of Changing Medical Technology* (ed. E. Chapman) (2002) *Community Genetics*; **5**(2), 110–19. ProQuest Medical Library.

Arksey, H. and Hirst, M. (2005) Unpaid carers' access to and use of primary care services. *Primary Health Care Research and Development*. **6**, 101–16.

Atherton, H. (2004) A history of learning disabilities, in *Learning Disabilities Towards Inclusion*, 4th edn (ed. B. Gates), Churchill Livingstone, London.

Atkinson, F. and Skarloff S. (1987) *Acute Hospital Wards and the Disabled Patient: A survey of the experience of patients and nurses*. Royal College of Nursing. London.

Barr, O., Gilgunn, J., Kane, T. and Moore, G. (1999) Health screening for people with learning disabilities by a community learning disability service in Northern Ireland. *Journal of Advanced Nursing*, **29**, 1482–91.

Beange, H., Lennox, N. and Parmenter, T. (1999) Health targets for people with an intellectual disability. *Journal of Intellectual and Developmental Disability*, **24**(4), 283–97.

Benson, L. (2004) Helping patients with learning disabilities, *GP Business*. 12 July 2004.

Binnie, A. and Titchen, A. (2001) *Freedom to Practise the Development of Patient-centred Nursing* Butterworth Heinemann. Oxford.

Bolton, J. (2003) Code of Ethics for Social Work at www.basw.co.uk – accessed January 2006.

Bond, L., Kerr, M., Dunstan, F. and Thapar, A. (1997) Attitudes of general practitioners towards health care for people with intellectual disability and the factors underlying these attitudes. *Journal of Intellectual Disability Research*, **41**, 391–400.

Broughton, S. and Thomson, K. (2000) Women with learning disabilities: Risk behaviours and experiences of the cervical smear test. *Journal of Advanced Nursing*, **32**, 905–12.

The Carers (Recognition and Services) Act 1995. HMSO. London.

The Carers (Equal Opportunities) Act 2004. HMSO. London.

Carers and Disabled Children Act 2000. HMSO. London.

Carter, G. and Jancar, J. (1983) Mortality in the mentally handicapped: a 50 year survey at the Stoke Park group of hospitals (1930–1980). *Journal of Mental Deficiency Research*, **27**, 143–56.

Cassidy, G., Martin, D.M., Martin, G.H.B. and Roy, A. (2002) Health checks for people with learning disabilities. *Journal of Learning Disabilities*, **6**(2), 123–36.

CHANGE Picture Bank and CHANGE Health Picture Bank. www.changepeople.co.uk

Chapman, E., (2002) Difficult decisions: Social and ethical implications of changing medical technology. *Community Genetics*, **5**(2), 110–19. ProQuest Medical Library.

College of Occupational Therapists. www.cot.org.uk accessed March 2006.

Commission for Social Care Inspection. (2006) www.csci.gov.uk accessed March 2006.

Corbett, J., Thomas, C., Prior, M. and Robson, R., (2003) Health facilitation for people with learning disabilities. *British Journal of Community Nursing*, **8**(9), 404–10.

Craft, A., Bicknell J. and Hollins, S. (1985) *Mental Handicap*. Bailliere Tindall, London.

Davis, J. (2005) Learning with families: Involving families in staff training. *Tizard Learning Disability Review*, **10**(3) 12–17.

Davis, S. and Marsden, R. (2001) Disabled people in hospital: Evaluating the CNS role. *Nursing Standard*, February **7**(15) 21.

Department of Constitutional Affairs. (2006) Mental Capacity Bill: Draft Code of Practice. www.dca.gov.uk/menincap/mcbdraftcode.pdf accessed Feb 2006.

Department of Health (1998) *Signposts for Success in Commissioning and Providing Health Services for People with Learning Disabilities*. (Main author: Lindsey, M.) NHS Executive. London.

Department of Health (1999a) *Caring about Carers: A National Strategy for Carers*. Department of Health. London.

Department of Health (1999b) *Once A Day* Main author: Lindsey, M., and Russell, O. NHS Executive. London.

Department of Health (2000) The NHS Plan: A plan for reform, a plan for investment. Department of Health. London.

Department of Health (2001a) *Good Practice in Consent Implementation Guide*. Department of Health. London. also at www.dh.gov.uk/consent.

Department of Health (2001b) *Planning with People: Towards person centered approaches Guidance for Partnership Boards*. Department of Health. London.

Department of Health (2001c) *Valuing People: A new strategy for learning disability for the 21st century*. Department of Health. London.

Department of Health (2002) *Action for Health – Health Action Plans and Health Facilitation; Detailed Good Practice Guidance on Implementation for Learning Disability Partnership Boards*. Department of Health, London.

Department of Health (2003a) *Delivering Investment in General Practice. Implementing the new GMS contract*. Department of Health. London.

Department of Health (2003b) *Fair for all Personal to you – Choice, Responsiveness and Equity in the NHS and Social Care.* A National Consultation. Department of Health. London.

Department of Health (2005a) *Five a Day: Eat more fruit and vegetables, easy read.* Department of Health. London.

Department of Health and Department for Education and Skills (2005b) *Carers and Disabled Children Act 2000 and Carers (Equal Opportunities) Act 2004 Combined Policy Guidance.* Department of Health. London.

Department of Health (2006) *Our Health, Our Care, Our Say: A new direction for community services.* Department of Health. London.

Department of Health/NHS Confederation/NHS Appointments Commission. (2005) *Promoting Equality and Human Rights in the NHS – A Guide for Non-Executive Directors of NHS Boards.* London.

DHSS (1971) *Better Services for the Mentally Handicapped.* HMSO. London.

Dicsfeld, K. (2001) Disability Matters in Medical Law. *Journal of Medical Ethics.* London. **27**(6) 388–92.

Dimond, B. (2005) *Legal Aspects of Nursing,* 4th edn, Pearson Longman. London.

Disability Discrimination Act (1995). HMSO. London.

Disability Rights Commission (2002) *Disability Discrimination Act 1995: Code of Practice, Rights of Access to Goods, Facilities, Services and Premises.* DRC, London.

Disability Rights Commission (2005) *Equal treatment: Closing the gap.* interim report of a formal investigation into health inequalities. www.drc-gb.org.

Dix, T. Gilbert, T. (1995) Informed Consent, in Gilbert, T. Todd, M. Practice issues in health settings. Routledge. London.

Djuretic, T., Laing-Morton, T., Guy, M. and Gill, M. (1999) Cervical screening for women with learning disability. Concerted effort is needed to ensure these women use preventive services. *British Medical Journal,* **318**, 536.

Doherty, C. (2003) in *Contemporary learning disability practice,* (eds M. Jukes and M. Bollard), Quay Books, Wiltshire.

Doody, G.A., Johnstone, E.C., Sanderson, T.L. *et al.* (1998) 'Pfropfschizophrenie' revisited: Schizophrenia in people with mild learning disability. *British Journal of Psychiatry,* **173**, 145–53.

Down's Syndrome Association (2004) *Schedule of Health Checks – Adults with Down's Syndrome.* London.

Duff, M., Scheepers, M., Cooper, M. *et al.* (2001) Helicobcter Pylori: Has the killer escaped from the institution? A possible cause of increased stomach cancer in a population with Intellectual disability. *Journal of Intellectual Disability,* **45**(3) 219–25.

Elliott, K. and Dean, E. (2004) *Traffic Light Assessment Tool,* Gloucestershire Partnership NHS Trust. Gloucester.

Emerson, E. (2001) Challenging behaviour: Analysis and intervention in *People with Severe Intellectual Disabilities,* 2nd edn, Cambridge: Cambridge University Press.

Evans, J., Mir, G., Atkin, K. *et al.* (2005) Identifying people with learning disabilities in general practice. *Living Well.* **5**(3) 18–22, Pavillion.

Ferris-Taylor (2002) in *Learning Disabilities Towards Inclusion,* 4th edn (ed. B. Gates), Churchill Livingstone, London.

Foundation for People with Learning Disabilities (2004) *Green Light Tool Kit, how good are your mental health services for people with learning disabilities?* a service improvement toolkit.

Fragile X Society. www.fragilex.org.uk accessed October 2005.

Gates, B. and Wilberforce, D. (2002) The nature of learning disabilities, in *Learning Disabilities Towards inclusion* 4th edn (ed. B. Gates) Churchill Livingstone. London.

Gilbert, P. (2000) *A–Z of Syndromes and Inherited Disorders,* 3rd edn, Stanley Thornes, Great Britain.

Gillman, M., Heyman, B., Swan, J. (2000) What's in a name? The implications of diagnosis for people with learning difficulties. *Disability and Society,* **15**(3) 389–409.

Giraud-Saunders, A., Gregory, M., Poxton, R. *et al.* (2003) *Valuing Health for All: Primary care trusts and the health of people with learning disabilities.* Institute for Applied Health and Social Policy, Kings College, London.

Glasby, A M. (2002) Meeting the needs of people with learning disabilities in Acute Care. *British Journal Of Nursing* **11**, No 21.

Grossman, S.A., Richards, C.F., Anglin, D. and Hutson, H.R. (2000) Caring for the patient with MR in the emergency department. *Annals of Emergency Medicine,* **35**(1), 69–76.

Guha, S. (1998) Health. Down's babies denied life-saving operations. BBC Here and Now. http://news.bbc.co.uk/1/hi/health/latest news/104480.stm.

Hansard Debate (2000) House of Commons Hansard Debate, Down's Syndrome. July 4th. www.parliament.the-stationary-office.co.uk accessed November 2005.

Harrison, S., Plant, A. and Berry, L. (2004) Valuing people: Developing health visiting practice for people with learning disabilities. *Practice Development in Health Care,* **3**(4), 210. Whurr. London.

Hassiotis, A., Barron, P. and O'Hara, J. (2000) Mental health services for people with learning disabilities: A complete overhaul is needed with strong links to mainstream services. *British Medical Journal,* **321**, 583–4.

Health Scotland (2002) *Keep Yourself Healthy* Series. Fair Multi media. Health Scotland. Edinburgh.

Hollins, S. and Wilson, J. (2004) *Looking after my Balls.* Gaskell. London.

Hollins, S., Attard, M.T., von Fraunhofer, N. and Sedgwick, P. (1998) Mortality in people with learning disability: Risks, causes, and death certification findings in London. *Developmental Medicine and Child Neurology,* **40**, 50–6.

Houghton, B. (2001) Caring for people with Down syndrome in A&E, *Emergency Nurse,* May 2001, **9**(2) 24.

Howells, G. (1986) Are the healthcare needs of mentally handicapped adults being met? *Journal of the Royal College of General Practitioners,* **36**, 449–53.

Human Rights Act (1998). HMSO, London.

Hurd, A. (2002) Development of pre-symbolic and pre-Linguistic skills, in *Management of Communication Needs in People with Learning Disability* (eds S. Abudarham and A. Hurd) Whurr. London.

Illsley. R (1977) Health and Social Policy – priorities for research. in Learning Disabilities Towards inclusion, 4th edn (ed. B. Gates) (2002) Churchill Livingstone. London.

Jackson E, Warner J. (2002) How much do doctors know about consent and capacity? *Journal of Royal Society of Medicine* **95**: 601–3.

Jay, P. (1979) *Report of the Committee of Enquiry into Mental Handicap Nursing and Care.* HMSO. London.

Keeley, B. and Clarke, M. (2003) *Primary Carers – Identifying and providing support to carers in primary care.* The Princess Royal Trust for Carers. London.

Kerr, M.. Dunstan, F. and Thapar, A. (1996) Attitudes of general practitioners to people with a learning disability. *British Journal of General Practice,* **46**, 92–4.

Keywood, K., Fovargue, S. and Flynn, M. (1999) *Best Practice? Health Care Decision-Making By, With and For Adults with Learning Disabilities.* National Development Team, Manchester.

Keywood, K. and Flynn, M. (2003) Healthcare decision making by adults with imtellectual disabilities: some levers to changing practice. *Psychiatry;* **2**, 8 or at www.intellectualdisability.info/values/decision_kk.html (Aug 05).

Knight, S.J.L. Regan, R. Nicod A. *et al.* (1999) Subtle chromosomal rearrangements in children with unexplained mental retardation. *Lancet* **345** (9191):1676–81.

The Law Commission (1991) Decision Making and the Mentally Incapacitated Adult. *Consultation Paper No. 119,* HMSO. London.

The Law Commission (1995) *Mental Incapacity Report. No. 231.* The Stationary Office. London.

Lennox, N. and Diggens, J. (1999) Knowledge, skills and attitudes: Medical schools coverage of an ideal curriculum on intellectual disability. *Journal of Intellectual and Developmental Disability,* **24**(4) 341–7.

Lennox, N.G. and Kerr, M.P. (1997) Primary health care and people with an intellectual disability: The evidence base. *Journal of Intellectual Disability Research,* **41**(5), 365–72.

Leyshon, S. and Clarke, L. (2005) Legal and ethical issues in seeking consent of adults with learning disability. *British Journal of Neuroscience Nursing.* **1**(3), 126–31.

Lothian University Hospitals trust with Lothian Primary Care Trust (2002) *A Collaborative Approach to Caring for Patients with a Learning Disability in the Acute Hospital.* Lothian University Hospitals Trust with Lothian Primary Care Trust. Edinburgh.

Martin, G., Axon, V. and Baillie, S. (2004) A joint practice nurse/community learning disability nurse annual health check for primary care patients with learning disabilities. *Learning Disability Practice* **7**(9), 30–3.

Makaton vocabulary project (2005) http://www.makaton.org.

McConkey, R. and Truesdale, M. (2000) Reactions of nurses and therapists in mainstream health services to contact with people who have learning disabilities. *Journal of Advanced Nursing* **32**(1), 158–63.

McGrother, C.W., Hauck, A., Bhaumik, S. *et al.* (1996) Community care for adults with learning disability and their carers: needs and outcomes from the Leicestershire register. *Journal of Intellectual Disability Research* **40**, 183–90.

Mencap, (2004) *Treat me Right, Better Healthcare for People with a Learning Disability.* Mencap, London.

Mental Capacity Act (2005) HMSO, London.

Mental Deficiency Act (1913) HMSO, London.

Mental Health Act (1959) HMSO, London.

Mental Health Act (1983) HMSO, London.

Messent, P.R., Cooke, C.B. and Long, J. (1998) Physical activity, exercise and health of adults with mild and moderate learning disabilities. *British Journal of Learning Disabilities,* **26**, 17–22.

Mitchell, D. (2000) in Brigham, L., Atkinson, D., *et al. Crossing Boundaries, Change and Continuity in the History of Learning Disability* (eds L. Brigham, D. Atkinson *et al.*) BILD. Kidderminster.

Moss, S.C., Prosser, H., Ibbotson, B. and Goldberg, D.P. (1996) Respondent and informant accounts of psychiatric symptoms in a sample of patients with learning disability. *Journal of Intellectual Disability Research,* **40**, 457–65.

Mueller, R. F. and Young, I. D. (1998) Emery's Elements of Medical Genetics, 10th edn., Churchill Livingstone, Edinburgh.

NHS Cancer Screening Programmes (2000) *Good practice in breast and cervical screening for women with learning disabilities.* NHSBSP/CSP. Sheffield. www.cancerscreening.nhs.uk.

NHS Careers (2006) www.nhscareers.nhs.uk. Accessed Jan 2006.

NHS Employers (2006) Revisions to the GMS contract 2006/2007 Delivering Investment in General Practice. NHS Employers. www.nhsemployers.org/primary/index.cfm accessed March 2006.

NHS Information Authority (2005) www.nhsia.nhs.uk/terms/pages/readcodes_intro. asp accessed March 2006.

National Council for Civil Liberties (1951) *50,000 Outside the Law: An examination of the treatment of those certified as mentally defective.* NCCL, London.

Parish A. and Markwick A. (1998) Equity and access to health care for women with learning disabilities. *British Journal of Nursing,* **7**, 92–6.

Parkes, N. (1996) Healthcare rationing for people with learning disabilities. *Nursing Standard,* **25**(11), 36–8.

Pritchard, P. (2003) in (2003) *Contemporary Learning Disability Practice* (eds M. Jukes and M. Bollard) Quay Books. Wiltshire.

Robertson, J., Emerson, E., Gregory, N. *et al.* (2000) Lifestyle related risk factors for poor health in residential settings for people with intellectual disabilities. *Research in Developmental Disabilities*, **21**, 469–86.

Roy, M., Clarke, D., Roy, A., ed (2000) An Introduction to learning disability psychiatry. www.ldbook.co.uk accessed October 2005.

Roy, A., Martin, D.M. and Wells, M.B. (1997) Health gain through screening – mental health: developing primary health care services for people with an intellectual disability (1). *Journal of Intellectual and Developmental Disability*, **22**, 227–39.

Royal National Institute of the Blind (2000) Minimising problems in eye surgery in people with severe learning disabilities. www.rnib.org.uk/welcome.htm Accessed August 2005.

Stein, K. (2000) Caring for people with learning disability: A survey of general practitioners' attitudes in Southampton and South-West Hampshire. *British Journal of Learning Disabilities*, **28**, 9–15.

Thompson, I.E., Melia, K.M. and Boyd, K.M. (2000) *Nursing Ethics*. Churchill Livingstone, London.

Valuing People Support Team (2002) Review of the role and function of Community Learning Disability Teams. www.valuingpeople.gov.uk/PartnershipPapers.htm.

Valuing People Support Team (2004) Update on Read Codes. www.valuingpeople.gov.uk/HealthPrimary.htm accessed February 2006.

Valuing People Support Team (2005) Traffic light assessment tool, Gloucestershire Partnership NHS Trust. www.valuingpeople.gov.uk/HealthHospital.htm.

Van Schrojenstein Lantaman-De Valk, H., Metsemakers, J.F., Haveman, M.J. and Crebolder, H.F. (2000) Health problems in people with intellectual disability in general practice: a comparative study. *Family Practice*, **17**(5):405–7.

Wallace, R., Schluter, P., Forgan-Smith, R. and Webb, P. (2003) Diagnosis of Helicobacter pylori infection in adults with intellectual disability. *Journal of Clinical Microbiology*. American Society for Microbiology, **41**(10), 4700–04.

Watson, D. (2002) in *Learning Disabilities Towards Inclusion*, 4th edn (ed. B. Gates) Churchill Livingstone. London.

While, A. (2004) Learning Disabilities: Lots of room for improvement. *British Journal of Community Nursing*, **9**(7), 310.

Whittaker, S. (2004) Hidden learning disability, *British Journal of Learning Disabilities*, BILD Publications, **32**, 139–43.

Wilson, D. and Haire, A. (1990) Health care screening for people with mental handicap living in the community. *British Medical Journal*, **301**, 1379–81.

World Health Organization (1992) Classification of Mental and Behavioural Disorders. *The ICD-10*. World Health Organization. Geneva.

Index